Why Can't There Be Peace in the World?

Why Can't There Be Peace in the World?

Children's Questions for God

Dr. Pat Fosarelli

ROWMAN & LITTLEFIELD
Lanham • Boulder • New York • London

Published by Rowman & Littlefield
An imprint of The Rowman & Littlefield Publishing Group, Inc.
4501 Forbes Boulevard, Suite 200, Lanham, Maryland 20706
www.rowman.com

86-90 Paul Street, London EC2A 4NE

British Library Cataloguing in Publication Information Available

Library of Congress Cataloging-in-Publication Data

Names: Fosarelli, Patricia D., author.
Title: Why can't there be peace in the world? : children's questions for God / Dr.
   Pat Fosarelli.
Description: Lanham : Rowman & Littlefield, [2024] | Includes bibliographical
   references and index.
Identifiers: LCCN 2024008123 (print) | LCCN 2024008124 (ebook) | ISBN
   9781538195970 (cloth) | ISBN 9781538195987 (ebook)
Subjects: LCSH: God (Christianity)—Juvenile literature. | God
   (Christianity)—Miscellanea.
Classification: LCC BT107 .F69 2024 (print) | LCC BT107 (ebook) | DDC
   231–dc23/eng/20240329
LC record available at https://lccn.loc.gov/2024008123
LC ebook record available at https://lccn.loc.gov/2024008124

To all the children and teens who expanded my understanding of God and my understanding of them.

Contents

Introduction

As a child, I was very interested in God and why God did the things God did. That meant that I asked a lot of questions about God . . . directed to anyone who I thought would have the answers! Naturally, my parents were on the front line in this regard, but my teachers and clergy were also recipients of these innocent questions. What was God *really* like? Why is the world the way it is? Does God like the way the world turned out, or does it make God sad? With my burgeoning child-like spirituality, the questions about God seemed endless.

Eventually, I addressed questions to God directly, especially when the adults in my life were unable (or unwilling) to engage in nonstop question answering. I thought that it was amazing that there was this Supreme Being that knew everything and could do anything. Surely God wouldn't mind humoring me by letting me ask whatever came to my mind.

As parents well know, children like to ask questions. Nonstop and repetitive questions can get tiresome sometimes, especially when a parent is busy or is occupied by adult matters. But asking questions is the way that children learn, and, as such, it's a given when living with, teaching, or working with children.

In fact, a few years ago, there was a television program called *Kids Say the Darndest Things*, in which children answered questions that the host asked them. Usually, their responses were hilarious, as they gave their own impressions about the world and how it should be. The times were more innocent then, and only a few children gave answers that weren't cute and entertaining.

Eventually, I grew up, but the questions never left me. As a pediatrician at Johns Hopkins and a pastoral theologian, I have heard my share of funny comments from children, when they were intentionally being funny and when they were unintentionally humorous. Yet, in both of my fields, I have also listened to children as they struggled to make meaning of the world, especially when they are ill, frightened, or experiencing loss. Their comments—and often questions—were anything but humorous, as they sought to understand the situations in which they found themselves. As I listened to them, I thought about my own innocent—but personally meaningful—questions long ago and far away. As I listened to them, I was frequently at a loss as to how to answer their questions or to respond to their comments.

For that reason, when I was working on my doctorate in ministry in the Baltimore-Washington area, I chose as the theme for my thesis the spiritual development of children in health and illness. At the time, I was working as a pediatrician in a clinic for children with terminal illnesses. Adults wanted to be supportive, but they often did not know how to answer the profound questions these children posed: "Why am I so sick? Why must I die when I haven't even grown up yet? Does God hear my prayers? Why won't God make me all better? Why does God let some people be sick and others be well? Am I being punished for something bad I did?" It was a lonely place for these children, as the adults in their lives didn't want them to dwell on questions about their illness or impending death; so the adults ignored or dismissed the questions. Yet, the questions were there nonetheless and didn't go away. Even professionals in the medical, nursing, social work, or ministry fields were unsure of what to say or whether to just ignore the questions, pretending not to hear them.

But I heard the children's questions.

I saw the look in their eyes when adults walked away, told them that they were being silly, or to "hush!" when they (the adults) couldn't bear to hear any more questions.

In all honesty, this was a "full-circle" time for me. When I was in medical school, I abandoned my faith because I couldn't come to terms as to how a good God would let innocent infants, children, and teens suffer. Nothing I learned in my years of religious education prepared me for what I saw on a daily basis—children with congenital malformations that would only bring them suffering and death; children with unrelenting diseases, the treatment of which was even harsher than the diseases; children with broken bones and spirits inflicted by the very people who should have loved them the most. I was pretty angry at God (if there was one) and even more positive that I didn't want a relationship with such a God. I became an agnostic—and a cynical one at that.

Ten years passed. By that time, I was a young attending pediatrician at Hopkins. As I rounded with students, interns, and residents, discussing medical issues, I was flummoxed by the experience of having children ask me "God questions" from their beds—despite the fact that I was not wearing any clothing or jewelry with religious significance. "Dr. Pat, do you think God wants me to be so sick? Dr. Pat, do you think God likes it when they have to keep sticking me to get an IV in? Dr. Pat, does God hear my prayers?" It was incredibly disconcerting for me. I knew that I could not answer in the way I felt ("Listen, kid, I don't even know if there is a God.") but that I also could not lie or avoid the questions. Instead, I learned to listen well, admit when I didn't know an answer, and let the children talk and ask their questions. In the process, I learned to be a faithful witness for them in the world, to allow them to speak when no one else would give them that permission.

So, years later, when it was time to propose a doctoral project in ministry (DMin), I wanted to bring my medical life and my faith life together in some way. I wanted to learn more about what's *really* on children's minds when they are so ill. Hence, I decided to ask them. I devised a simple, seven-question, open-ended questionnaire that children could answer anonymously, listing only their gender and their age. The questions were straightforward ones about God and God's relationship to the world. I crafted the questionnaire as open-ended, because I didn't know how children would respond to the questions. Rather than give them multiple choices (and potentially force them to choose an answer that they really wouldn't have chosen), I chose to let them speak for themselves. Initially, I was only going to offer the questionnaire to the children in the clinic, but I wondered how children not impacted by a life-threatening illness would answer the same questions. In the end, I asked both healthy children and ill children to complete the questionnaire. By the time I completed my thesis, about one hundred children had completed it.

Once awarded the DMin degree, I could have stopped distributing the questionnaires, but I didn't. I was allowing children to have a voice, and I was learning so much. At the time, I offered many presentations about child development, childcare, and children's issues to parents, teachers, and ministers in the Baltimore-Washington area, with the most commonly requested presentation one that focused on the spiritual development of children and teens. Prior to giving the presentation, I got into the habit of asking those who invited me if they would like a generic talk on their chosen topic or if they would like the talk tailored to their own children's reported experiences and development. Everyone to whom that question was addressed opted for the latter and agreed to having their children complete the questionnaires. Parents (and teachers) could see the questionnaire before it was offered to the children, but they were cautioned not to coach their children ahead of time as to "right" answers . . . because they are no right answers. Since most children in the United States are from Christian denominations, the questionnaire was given to children of various Christian faith traditions at churches and schools (and occasionally community sites). They answered the questionnaire on their own. Although different denominations were represented, with few exceptions, children of comparable ages and gender answered questions more similarly than differently.

Now, years later, over nine thousand children have completed the questionnaire, and I have a much better idea of how children think about God and the world. Given that the questionnaires were completed by children who wrote their answers, not every questionnaire was legible, yet unreadable/unusable questionnaires were in the minority.

I wrote this book for all the parents and teachers who have asked me, "How would you answer *this* question?" over my years in ministry and medicine. In doing so, I wanted to present both the common and the profound questions that are on the minds of children and teens, with the realization that sometimes the common and the profound are one and the same. I also wanted to offer ways of answering the questions that would give parents and those who work with young people some assistance with how to respond to the question so that greater communication would result. Even though the questions presented in this book were originally addressed to God, many of them are not at all religious questions (e.g., "Why do human beings do bad things?"). For that reason, the suggestions offered can apply across a variety of topics and concerns.

In this book, I will focus on only one question in the seven-question survey: "If you could ask God one question (and get it answered), what one question would you ask God?" In responding to this question, children permit adults to better understand what insights they have about the God to whom they pose their questions.

In many cases, the questions the children have for God are the same that adults might pose. Why must there be illness and death? Why must we suffer? Why does it seem that the good suffer more than the wicked? From where does evil come? In addition, many children's questionnaires were marked by a "theme." For example, if the question to God was about evil, then it was likely that the theme of evil was expressed in their responses to other questions on the original questionnaire as well.

The top eight categories of questions for God submitted by the children were selected for this book. These categories are questions about (1) God; (2) the children themselves; (3) loved ones, usually parents and siblings; (4) human beings in general; (5) evil and suffering; (6) illness, suffering, and death; (7) nature and creation; and (8) heaven.

Each of these eight themes has a chapter. In the chapter, I present a sample of questions relating to that theme, providing the age and gender of the child or teen who asked the question. These questions can act as springboards for discussion with children. For example, we can say, "Some children wonder what God looks like. What do you think?" Then, general suggestions are provided for answering the sub-theme questions; for example, in the section on evil, there are subsections on human-made evil, natural disasters, etc. The suggestions are grouped by age: five to eight years, nine to twelve years, and adolescents. These categories were chosen because the types of responses given were similar among children in these groupings. Finally, sample conversations between a child of each age group and an adult focusing on an actual question submitted by one of the children is provided to give the reader a model on how to handle certain topics.

Unlike other books about children's questions to God, this book is not meant to be cute and funny, although some of what the children ask might strike us as humorous. Instead, it is meant to help us answer the questions children have for God—and for us. By knowing the most common questions children pose to God, we have a better sense of what is on their minds. That, in turn, might help us to respond to the questions children pose to us.

Chapter 1

How Children Think
and Believe

This book covers questions asked by young people between the ages of five and seventeen. To better understand their responses, we do well to understand the way they think in general and about God in particular.

HOW CHILDREN THINK AND BELIEVE BY AGE

In my descriptions of how children think, I will be relying on work done by the Swiss psychologist Jean Piaget, who was interested in how children and adolescents developed their abilities to reason.[1] In my descriptions of how children relate to others, I will refer to the work done by the psychologist Erik Erikson, who was interested in how human beings of all ages relate to the world, other people, and themselves.[2] Finally, in my descriptions of how children come to faith, I am indebted to the work of James Fowler, a psychologist and an ordained minister, who both hypothesized how human beings come to belief and verified his hypotheses by interviewing people of all ages.[3]

---

1. Dorothy Singer and Tracey Revenson, *A Piaget Primer: How Children Think* (New York: New American Library, 1996).

2. Erik Erikson, "Eight Stages of Man," in *Childhood and Society* (New York: W. W. Norton, 1985).

3. James Fowler, Stages of Faith: *The Psychology of Human Development and the Quest for Meaning* (New York: HarperOne, 1995).

Five Years Old

There were very few five-year-olds in this project, but their inclusion requires a comment. Although five-year-olds are almost of elementary school age, they are still, strictly speaking, preschoolers. Preschoolers think in very imaginative ways. They are unable to grasp adult logic and so they invent their own "logic" to explain what goes on around them. Jean Piaget called this stage *preoperational.* For preschoolers, *anything* is possible. After all, if they can believe that a single rotund man gets to everyone's house in the world on Christmas Eve to deliver gifts, or if they can believe that a large rabbit delivers baskets of candy on Easter morning, they can believe anything.

Their ideas about God may, at times, seem profound; in other words, they have many intuitions about God that we adults simply do not have. On the other hand, they often project on to God the attitudes, words, and actions of those closest to them (e.g., their parent[s]), since they believe parental figures to be powerful. James Fowler called this faith stage *intuitive-projective.* Preschoolers believe that God has magical powers, powers that the powerless children lack. Yet, they also believe that God is like them, enjoying games, pizza, and candy. They wonder who God's mother and father are and whether God has siblings.

Six to Eight Years Old

In the younger elementary school years (ages 6 to 8), the culture of formal schooling leads children to believe that a question or problem has only one right answer, although many wrong answers are possible. After all, numbers that are added can only have one correct answer, and words can have only one correct spelling. Children at this age are not good at ambiguities and gray areas. In their never-ending quest to figure out the adult world, they seek the right answers so that they will seem more grown-up. Furthermore, they learn best at this age with concrete objects to reinforce the lesson. For example, teachers teach adding and subtracting with pennies or pieces of candy to demonstrate concretely what "7" or "12" looks like. Children copy spelling words on paper to learn them better. Students trace their fingers over maps to learn about the relative size of countries in the world. Piaget called this stage *concrete operations.*

Their ideas about God are also concrete. God is depicted as an old man, a young man with a beard, or a white bird. They learn from

Scripture stories about the heroes and heroines of the Christian faith tradition, and they want no creative deviation from those stories. They want the facts because anything else can be confusing. Yet, they also delight in stories about superheroes and superheroines, stories in which the bad guys get what's coming to them. They want stories in which good overcomes evil, stories in which the moral of the story is that good is always stronger than evil. Fowler called this stage *mythic-literal*. Because children are so literal, their questions to God are frequently the same, and the answers that they hope to receive would also be concrete.

For example, children of this age are very concerned about prayers that are not answered. If God is our best friend, why doesn't God act like a best friend and help us when we need it? The children know that their own best friends help when they need it. Because children of this age base their expectations of the behavior of best friends on their own experiences, it is no wonder that they think this way. Furthermore, in their estimation, the answer to the question of why God doesn't answer prayers is rather straightforward. God doesn't answer prayers for someone because God is mad at her (just like her mom), too busy (just like her dad), or trying to teach a lesson (just like her teacher).

Nine to Twelve Years Old

In the older elementary school and preteen years, many children are still thinking literally and concretely, although toward the end of this age grouping, young people are thinking in more abstract terms, at least occasionally. Furthermore, older children in this age group are now better able to see the gray areas or ambiguities about life, making discussions a valuable form of teaching at this age. Piaget would say that these older children are moving toward the stage of *formal operations*, the adult way of thinking.

With respect to God, while the younger children in this age group are in the *mythic-literal* stage, older children are in the Fowler stage called *synthetic-conventional*. Synthetic means bringing together, making, while conventional is the usual, the norm, the expected. Most children identify with the faith tradition in which they have been raised. Yet, because of their increasingly greater independence, they are coming into contact with children and adults whose religious beliefs do not match those of themselves or their parents. Just a few short years earlier, they were so sure of their religious beliefs, but now some questions arise. Is there really a God? Why do different people have different rituals and houses of worship? Who is right in their beliefs? From the certainty of their earlier years, they are now in the relative confusion of the preteen years, and they seek answers. The questions of these young people reflect their greater cognitive sophistication; their questions are not those of their younger siblings. But they are also not those of their more sophisticated older siblings either.

For example, children of this age might ask God why he made human beings if he knew ahead of time what human beings would do to the earth and to each other. They might ask why people who do bad things are allowed to keep doing what they are doing. On a more personal note, they might want to know why they were put on this earth or why God made them the way they are.

Adolescents

With their ever-increasing fund of knowledge, ability to think abstractly, and willingness to ask the hard questions, adolescents are keenly interested in why the world is in the shape it is in, why human beings treat each other badly, and why certain people seem to suffer more than their share. No longer hoping for easy answers, adolescents are more interested in pressing both adults and God for answers that are real, albeit unpleasant, and they might do so by posing hypothetical situations. This is in keeping with their more adult way of thinking, Piaget's stage of *formal operations*.

Fowler called their stage *individuative-reflective*. Adolescents must begin to come to terms with what they believe, and this is a very individual task. No one can do it for anyone else. Furthermore, it takes much reflection and interior work. Young people are usually not entirely through this process by the end of adolescence, as they continue to struggle with the thorny issues of their lives and time. If truth be told, many adults are in this stage as well.

Their questions for God have either an almost plaintive quality ("Why do you let people suffer?") or an angry one ("Why don't you help those who need help? Don't you care?"). Their questions are not the easy ones of their childhood but the painful ones of their lived experience as members of their family and citizens of the world. The answers they seek are not those sought by younger children (i.e., a cut-and-dried response once and for all). On the contrary, the answers they seek will, by necessity, lead to discussion and perhaps even more questions.

For example, adolescents have seen innocent people suffering, and they know it is wrong. If they know that it is wrong, surely God must know since God knows all. Why, then, does God permit it to continue? If they were in God's place, they are certain that they would not permit it. So, what is the purpose of suffering?

GENERAL GUIDELINES FOR ADDRESSING CHILDREN'S AND TEENS' QUESTIONS

Regardless of the question asked, several general guidelines for addressing them are in order:

Listen Carefully

Many times, children and teens talk so much or so rapidly that we adults tune them out. Although that is understandable, it is certainly not the tact to take if we really want to engage young people in meaningful discussions. We need to listen carefully so that we can learn what the real issues are. Listening is done with the ears, brain, eyes, *and* heart, as it is important to detect what is not being said as well as what is. Furthermore, we need to listen before we formulate a response. In other words, we should not interrupt or hurry the young person along. Finally, our nonverbal body language should demonstrate that we are truly interested: making eye contact, leaning a bit forward (if possible), nodding of head, and so on. Ideally, such conversations are held in places where these are possible, but we must engage the questions wherever they occur . . . even when in the car!

If you hear any comments that are concerning, ask further questions gently. If any responses seem worrisome, seek professional guidance.

Ask Appropriate Questions

If a young person brings up an unusual question, it is good to ask him or her a question that acknowledges that it is an unusual one. This should be done in a nonjudgmental way. A good response to an unusual question is, "That's a great question. Why did that come up today?" In such a way, the child or teen will hear that you appreciate the question. It is also a good way to gauge what is going on in the child's mind or world.

Try to Avoid Yes-or-No Answers and Anything That Truncates the Conversation

A "yes" or "no" answer does not usually lead to discussion; neither do one-word answers. Furthermore, answers that imply frustration or anger at, or devaluation of the young person's question, are also communication stoppers. If we want young people to communicate with us, we need to be hospitable enough to give them our full attention and to take their questions and concerns seriously. Furthermore, we should do nothing that sends the message that the conversation is over, if it really is not.

Don't React to a Child's or Teen's Anger or Negative Feelings

Children and teens should not be permitted to hurt others in word or in action. Other than that, the child or teen should be allowed to state what is on his or her mind. Acting shocked (even if we are) is counterproductive. An adult's expression of shock discourages some young people from saying anything else, while it encourages other young people to escalate their ranting and raving just to see how upset the adult will become. The more we can resist the urge to prejudge the question or comment that the child or teen presents, the more likely it will be that greater communication will occur.

Don't Make Up Answers When You Really Don't Know—Always Be Willing to Say, "I Don't Know" if That's the Case

Although we might not know the response to a given question, it might be something that we can discover through some research (e.g., "How many people are on the earth?"). Other questions do not lend themselves to easily found answers (e.g., "Why did my friend Kimmy die?") Children and teens do not always expect us to have the answers. The best response to questions that have no "set" answers is, "I don't know. What do you think?" This is useful because it shows children and teens that they are not alone in their failure to understand the situation; we adults don't always understand situations either. It also gives us an opportunity to see if there are erroneous ideas at work. In the previous example, "Why did Kimmy die?" if an adult asks the young person what he or she thinks, and the answer is, "God hated Kimmy," that would be an opportunity to enter into a discussion both about God and about hatred. In other words, as the young person is encouraged to speak about the meaning of hate, he or she is invited to explore how that concept fits with his or her understanding of God.

Always Leave the Door Open for More Discussions

Many children and teens don't have all their questions neatly lined up; they must ponder them a bit. So, there should be no surprise when a child or teen revisits a topic after raising it in an earlier conversation; sometimes, this is done at the most inopportune times! When adults demonstrate a willingness to communicate and grapple with the hard issues that are troubling the children and adolescents in our midst, young people will feel safe and return over and over again to seek guidance or to debate certain points. If the timing is not right for a time for quality communication, it is better to say, "This issue is really important to me, as I know it is for you. But now is not the time for me to give you my full attention. Can we talk this evening?" Then, it's up to us to make sure that this happens. Broken promises do not encourage open communication.

Realize That You Also Can Grow as You Respond to the Young Person in Your Life

The more we are prompted to engage in meaningful dialogue with children and teens about hard issues, the more we will grow in our own understanding of ourselves and how we approach the mysteries of life. In addition, we are often encouraged to re-think our positions, based on the comments and questions that are presented by the young people in our lives. Often, we are so used to our own opinions about matters that we don't take the time to consider other ways of viewing a topic . . . until we are drawn into discussion with someone about whom we care very much.

HOW TO USE THIS BOOK

Naturally, like any book, this one can be read straight through, and for individuals who have an interest in knowing which issues concern children so much that they wish to ask God about them, this might be the way to use this book. Alternatively, sections of interest can be read and pondered, especially as one prepares to speak to a young person of a particular age. In such a situation, it *is* helpful to know what other children of that age wonder about. Regardless of the method, as one reads the examples of the children's questions for each section by age, one might imagine how a question could be answered if it were posed. Some questions are so profound that we find ourselves at a loss to formulate an adequate answer. Other questions concern issues about which we do not have easy answers at our fingertips, but we can learn the answers through a reputable source online or otherwise. Some questions may elicit tears, while others may evoke smiles.

Each chapter will begin with common questions posed by children in a given age group, although I may be quoting only one child's phrasing of a question. When direct quotes of questions are provided in this book, they will be followed by parentheses, which include a number (the child's age) and B or G (for boy or girl, respectively) to give the reader a sense of who actually posed each individual question that I am quoting. This same rule will be used in those chapters with subheadings. When sample questions are not provided for a particular age group, there were very few questions addressing that topic. Examples of questions that were posed but not used in a chapter are presented in the appendix.

My hope in writing this book (with the help of so many children and teens) is that communication between children and teens and the adults in their lives will be improved. Readers will see that the questions *they* have fielded from *their* children and teens are not unique; they are also posed by many other children and teens. I also hope that readers will get a glimpse of what I have been privileged to experience in both medicine and ministry—the joys and sorrows of communicating with children and adolescents in both the good times and the not so good times. In addition, for those readers who believe in God, I hope that the words of the children and teens, addressed to God, give renewed vitality to their own relationship with God.

Finally, a word about the use of gender pronouns with respect to God: Young children can only know what they see and hear around them. If they hear the name God associated with male pronouns, that is what they use, and, indeed, that is what was seen in the questionnaires. In other words, it's mostly taken for granted that God is male. As children become older, they learn that God has no gender; God is Spirit, although Jesus was certainly male while on earth. Questions about God's identity may arise at this time, especially in adolescence, and particularly when they hear Scripture passages with maternal imagery. For the purposes of this book, however, I will remain faithful to the children's wording in the responses provided.

Chapter 2

Children's Questions about God and God's Ways

REPRESENTATIVE QUESTIONS ABOUT GOD AND GOD'S WAYS FROM THE SURVEYS

(Note: The number and letter in parenthesis denote the age and gender of the child posing the question. When numbers are separated by a dash, children of the ages included posed that question.)

Five to Eight Years Old

Are you real? (5–8)
How old are you? (5–8)
Are you happy [huge]? (5–6)
What do you do all day? Do you work hard? (5–7)
Who is your mother and father? (8 G)
Do you have brothers and sisters? (8 G)

Nine to Twelve Years Old

Are you real? (9–12)
Who is your mother? (10 G)
Will we ever see you in person? [If you're with us, why can't we see you?] (11 G)
Are you a man or a woman? (12)

Thirteen Years and Older

Are you real? (13–15)
Why not appear to shut up non-believers once and for all? (13–17)

INTRODUCTION

Like human beings everywhere and throughout history, children and adolescents have an insatiable interest in God or a Supreme Being. Human beings have sought to understand God through nature, fellow human beings, and sacred texts. But definitive answers are hard to come by. Some religions think God is one with nature, while other religions posit a God wholly removed from nature. Some religions think we see God in those around us, while other religions hold that God is totally offended by humanity and is not identified with people in any way. Some religions believe that God speaks through sacred texts, while other religions believe that such texts have arisen from human imagination alone. Religions argue over which texts are truly sacred and authentic, and which are not.

For individuals (regardless of age) who believe in God, the divine cannot be entirely described by human language, and most attempts at doing so have come up lacking in some way. Children and teens strive to understand what adults have thought over time and think today about this God. Because young children are so concrete, they can only imagine God to be something or someone with whom or which they are familiar. To a young child, if God is described as "Father," for example, then God looks like any dad (or grandfather) does. If God is a spirit, maybe God looks like the ghost a child saw in a movie or cartoon. After all, to a young child, what does "God is a Spirit" really mean? Is God some kind of scary ghost, or is this Spirit friendly? Even more confusing is a statement like "God is love." What does that really mean in the everyday world? If I love my pet dog, is God in the pet dog?

Naturally, as children mature into adolescence, their ability to understand metaphors and imagery also matures, and they can understand "God is a Spirit" as something that is not a ghost. But what does it really mean? Even though older children and adolescents have a better appreciation of metaphors and imagery, such figures of speech only say what God is like, not necessarily what God is.

Truth be told, metaphors and imagery relating to God are confusing to many adults, as are attempts to explain God's attributes and God's ways. After all, what does it mean to say God had "no beginning"? How can that be possible? What does it mean to say God is "all-powerful" or "all-good"? If God is indeed all powerful, why doesn't God stop terrible or evil things from happening? If God is all good, why do innocent people suffer? Such questions relate to a field of theology called "theodicy," which grapples with God's role in why certain things occur. This will be discussed more fully in the section about children's questions as to why evil exists.

But if this seeming dichotomy between God's love (and power) and the obvious evil in the world (for example) are hard for us as adults to comprehend, it's even harder for those whose worldview is so much more limited. It doesn't seem fair or right. Some adults respond to this dichotomy by saying that there is no God or there's no proof of God, because what kind of God would let horrific things happen? Other people say human beings can never understand the mind of God, so we're in no position to question. Yet, those who believe in God must have some way of identifying the presence of God and saying something meaningful about God, especially to the children in their midst. In the best of times, we often stumble our way through an answer; in the worst of times, we're often simply at a loss for words.

WHAT THE SURVEYS REVEAL

Questions to God about God were the most frequent questions asked by the children and adolescents. (In fact, if we are honest, we would admit that we adults also have many questions about God!) Children and teens wonder about who God is and why God does the things he does. The younger children wonder more about God's abilities, while older children and teens are concerned as to why God does (or doesn't do) certain things. As children age, although they might still pose very concrete questions to God (e.g., "Who are your parents?"), there are fewer occurrences of them, because the complexity of the questions increases with each year.

Because there are so many questions in this category, for each age, topics will be discussed in question sub-categories.

QUESTIONS

God's Nature

Five to Eight Years Old

> *What's it like being God? (5–8)*
> *Do you pray for us? (5 G)*
> *Are you a cloud, or do you just live in one? (5 B)*
> *Do you bowl [sing, eat pizza]? (5)*
> *Who's your wife? (6 G)*
> *Do you have a middle and last name? (6 G)*
> *What's your real name? (8 B)*
> *Are you a head or a full body? (8 G)*
> *Why are you a bird? (8 G)*
> *Are you the only God? (8 B)*
> *How did you become God? (8 B)*
> *Do you have a God? (8 B)*

Nine to Twelve Years Old

> *Are you the real God? (10 B)*
> *How did you get the name God? (11 B)*
> *What do you do when you're not busy? (10 G)*
> *What is your full name? (11 G)*
> *Do you have a family? (10 B)*
> *Are you a man or a woman? (11 G)*
> *Are you black? (11 B)*
> *What are you made of? (11 G)*
> *What's your favorite prayer? (11 G)*
> *What is your best memory? (11 B)*
> *Would you do it all over again? (11 B)*
> *Is the world better now or way back then? (11 B)*
> *Who will succeed you if you ever die? (11 B)*
> *Do you know everyone individually in the world? (11 G)*
> *How were you alive before time? (12 B)*
> *Were you assigned to be God? [Who chose you?] (12 B)*
> *What do you like most about being God? (12 G)*
> *Do you pray for people? (12 G)*

Younger children are very interested in whether God is real and God's full name, age, appearance, relatives—parents, spouse, siblings—domicile, and friends. Other than if God is real, the other attributes are all ones that they want others to know about them. They also wonder if God always hears them, loves them, and is always with or watching over them. These young children want to know whether God is like the descriptions they have been taught and whether God is like them (e.g., "What games do *you* like to play?"). Very concrete in their approaches, their questions can strike us as amusing. An adult answering a child's questions about God should first discover what a child thinks is the answer and then share with him or her what the religious tradition says about God. For example, when a child asks whether God ever gets sleepy or sick (like children often do), the adult can remind the children that God is a spirit, not a human, and spirits do not become sick or sleepy. Furthermore, since God is perfect, God doesn't need sleep (because God is never tired).

Although several questions occur throughout the age range ("Are you real?" "Do you love everyone/everything that you made?" "Can you make people nicer?"), in general, the more profound questions are posed by older children, with an occasional one stated by a younger child, such as the one asked by a seven-year-old girl: "How does it feel to hear someone praying to you?"

On the other hand, some older children continue to ask the concrete questions posed by their younger counterparts (e.g., "Do you speak English?" "Who are your parents?"), but many ask questions that cannot be easily answered. "What's it like to be God?" "How did you become God?" "How can you have no beginning and no end?" "What was it like when it was all darkness?" These are questions that truly only God can answer. Older children have many of the same questions as do younger children, but they often phrase them with greater sophistication. Because they are at a higher cognitive level than are their younger counterparts, the answers that we provide can respect their ever-increasing maturity.

For example, to the question, "Who assigned you to be God?" we can respond that God was before anybody or anything that could have "assigned" him. Likewise, to the question "How were you alive before time?," we can answer that time is a human notion. Because God is eternal (always was, always will be), God can easily exist before the

notion of time was devised. Both of these questions tap into children's
wonderings about eternity. Although children can understand something
that is without end, they have a much harder time imagining something
without a beginning. To the question "What did you do before you
made everything?" we can encourage children to speculate a bit about
that question, noting that these are all good questions but ones that only
God can answer.

To the question "What are you made of?" we can respond that God
is a spirit, and a spirit is not material. Therefore, it cannot be made
of something. As a final example, to the question "Do you pray for
us?" (a very common question), we can explain what prayer is (communication with God). God has no need to communicate with himself.
Furthermore, there is no superior "god" to which God prays. Therefore,
God does not pray. What God does do is to communicate with people
by giving them insights and inspiration. We can encourage children and
teens to recall a time when they believed that God was giving them
inspiration or insights about a problem or something that was on their
minds. We might also share a time when we believed that God was
doing the same for us.

God's Perfection, Abilities, and Infinitude

Five to Eight Years Old

> *If you can do anything, can you tickle yourself? (5 G)*
> *Can you fly or go places fast? (6 B)*
> *How do you do it all [everything]? (7 B)*
> *How can you be everywhere at once? (7–11)*
> *How can you see and hear everyone at the same time? (7–11)*
> *What created you? (8 B)*
> *How do you know what everyone is doing? (8 B)*
> *How do you know everyone's name? (8 B)*
> *How do you help more than one person at a time? (8 G)*
> *How can you have no beginning and no end? (8 B)*
> *What was it like for you when it was all darkness? (8 G)*
> *How did you get your powers? (8 G)*
> *Can you die? Why not? (8 G)*

Nine to Thirteen Years Old

Are you good at everything? (9–10 B)
How were you born when no one was alive? (9 G)
Were you alive before the dinosaurs? (9 G)
Where did you come from? (9 G)
How do you do miracles? (10–12)
How can you be always perfect? (10 G)
How can you know [understand] everything? (11 G)
How do you do it all—it seems impossible to me? (11 B)
How did you make yourself? (12 G)
How is it possible for you to "be" at the beginning? (13 B)
How do you know everything there is to know? (10–13)

From the smile-evoking "Can you tickle yourself?" raised by one of the survey's youngest respondents to the profound "How can you already be at the beginning?" children and teens have many questions about God's abilities. Mostly, they are in awe, nicely captured by the question of an eleven-year-old, "How do you do it all—it seems impossible to me?"

Young children wonder how God can know everyone, can hear everyone's prayers at the same time, or help everyone who asks for help. When we consider the young child's experience, it is impossible for her to hear even both parents at one time, let alone siblings as well! She can only help one person at a time. These powers are simply unimaginable to children, as they should be to us adults as well. Adults responding to such questions can express their own amazement at such abilities.

The questions of older children are more probing than that of their younger counterparts. "Who inspired you to be holy?" "Who will succeed you if you die?" "Who assigned you to be God?" In responding to these questions, we can note that God is perfect, all good. Also, since God is limitless and eternal, God had no beginning, and God has no end. Thus, no one assigned God to be God, no one was God's inspiration for holiness, and there is no need for a successor to God, since God is infinite and cannot die.

Adolescents struggle to understand what they have been told about God. How is it possible for God to "be" at the beginning? How was God formed? Teens, especially those interested in science, cannot fathom how something could "be" before the beginning of time. Although teens can understand the concept of infinity going forward, they do not necessarily understand it going backward. Yet, "infinity" means limitless. The eternal nature of God is a difficult concept for all human beings to grasp, wedded as we are to the present. The same is true of the infinitude of God (especially God's limitless powers) because we are finite. How can one really know everything? How can one really hear everyone's prayers? The human mind rebels at such notions. Because only God can give accurate answers to many of these adolescent questions, we can commiserate with their bewilderment and engage in discussions as to what God is like.

Concerns about God

Five to Eight Years Old

> *How does it feel to hear someone praying to you? (7 G)*
> *Is it hard to be you? (8 G)*
> *Are you lonely? (8 G)*
> *What's your favorite thing to do with people? (8 B)*
> *Why do some people hate you? (8 G)*
> *What makes you happy? (7 B)*
> *Do you ever get sick or sleepy? Where do you sleep? (7 G)*
> *Can I pray for you? (8 B)*
> *Do you like being so popular? (8)*
> *What's it like to live in the clouds? (8 G)*
> *What do you love to do? (8 B)*
> *Do you like living so long? (8 B)*

Nine to Twelve Years Old

> *Are you happy [having fun]? (9 G)*
> *Do you get tired of being God? (9 G)*
> *Why do you keep forgiving? (9 G)*
> *Do you still love people when they mess up? (9 B)*
> *Are you upset when we don't say thanks? (9 B)*
> *How do you feel when people don't like you? (9 G)*
> *Do you like being learned about? (9 G)*
> *Do you enjoy being God? (10 B)*

Why don't some people trust you? (10 G)
How disappointed are you in the world? (10 G)
Is it hard being God? Do you like it? (multiple)
Is it hard when people don't believe in you? (12 G)
Are you disappointed in us? (12 B)

Adolescents

Why are you so generous [good to me]? (13 G)
Do you like the way your life has gone so far? (13 B)
How do you feel after all these years? (14 B)
Do you ever wish that people would ask about you? (16 G)

Some of the most touching questions are ones that children and teens raise about God's feelings. From the simple "Do you like being popular?" to the profound "Do you ever wish people would ask about you?" young people often regard God as very human. These questions, of course, have no answers that human beings can provide. Yet, each of these questions can provide wonderful material for a discussion about God, a discussion in which adults can learn to appreciate God in a new way, based on the insights of children and teens.

For example, to the question, "Is it hard being God?" or "Do you get tired of being God?" children and adults can discuss what seems to be the advantages of being God . . . and the disadvantages. To the question, "How does it feel to hear people praying to you?" children of all ages and adults can imagine what it's like to hear so many prayers and to know that they cannot all be answered. To the question, "Are you disappointed in us?" teens and adults can discuss the ways that human beings fall very short of the potential that God has given them. How would they feel if they were God?

God's Behavior

Have you ever been bad? (8 B)
How can you never sin? (8 G)
Do you cry when people sin? (8 G)
Have you ever made a mistake? (9 G)
Are you ever tempted to sin? (12 B)

Older children are beginning to struggle with their own tendencies to do things that are wrong, and they wonder how God can be consistently good, something which neither they nor their parents can be. "How can you never sin?" asked a bewildered eight-year-old. This is an opportunity to explain to children what "perfect" means and how human beings can be good but not perfect. Furthermore, in light of God's perfection, children wonder whether God cries when human beings are bad. Note that they do not ask whether God is angered by human beings but whether he is saddened by them. For many children and teens, how an all-good God can even permit evil is beyond their understanding (as it is for many adults as well). In other words, how can perfect goodness tolerate evil? A related concern is whether God made bad people. In responding to such questions and concerns, we can state that God does not make bad people, but people do bad things, a concept with which older children will have little difficulty. Furthermore, we can highlight God's love and mercy, reminding children that no matter what they do, God continues to love them.

God's Relationship to Creation

Five to Eight Years Old

> *Do you love everyone/everything that you've made? (all)*
> *Can you make dinosaurs [dragons] again? (6 B)*
> *Who helped you make the world? (7 G)*
> *How did you make the sun without burning your fingers? (7 B)*
> *Was it easy to make everyone unique? (8 G)*
> *How did you decide to make what you did? (8 G)*
> *What gave you the idea to create everything [the world]? (8)*
> *Was it hard to make the earth? (8 G)*

Nine to Twelve Years Old

> *Did you like creating the world? (9 G)*
> *Did you make all the planets? (11 G)*
> *What were you doing before creation? (11 G)*
> *Why did you make the world as it is? (11 G)*
> *Did you really make everything? (12 B)*
> *How did you make the world so quickly? (12 B)*

Adolescents

Would you create stuff differently? (13 B)
What was it like before everything else was created? (13 B)

While younger children are interested if God made certain things, older children are much more interested in the whys and hows. Again, these are questions that most adults cannot answer for certain. We can respond with God's imagination is endless, as are God's creative powers.

Older children are also very interested in how God created the world and God's continuing relationship with the world. Children see that the world is far from perfect, and since God is perfect, they surmise that God must be unhappy with the world, especially the actions of human beings. In response to these concerns, we can acknowledge that God is probably unhappy with some of the things that happen in the world, because God is love, and many bad things happen because of hate. We can, however, underscore God's continuing desire to love us and forgive us when we fall short of the mark, a good answer to the question posed by one child: "Do you still love people when they mess up?" We can also emphasize that God loves what has been created and wants it to be the best that it can be.

God's Relationship to Humankind

What do you love the most? (6–8 G)
Do you love everyone the same amount? (8 G)
What did you make that you love the most? (9 B)
Who do you really think is the best? (10 B)

Both younger and older children want to know if God loves everyone the same or whether God has favorites; for young children, love is a commodity that has limits. This is not a question that adolescents posed, which would be expected with adolescents' greater understanding that love is not limited. This question arises because in the children's experience, they frequently note that adults (parents, teachers, etc.) play favorites, preferring one child over another. We can remind children that God loves everyone, and that, unlike human beings, God does not have favorites because God is perfect.

Whom does God love the most? Many children hope that it is themselves! In response to this question, we can stress that God, indeed, loves everyone but certainly doesn't love the bad things that are done. God's love is infinite for each and every person.

God's Response to Prayers

Why don't you help those who need you and ask for help? (12 B)
Why don't you answer prayers in the way we want? (12 G)
Why do you answer some prayers and not others? (16 G)

The first question—"Why don't you answer prayers in the way we want?"—was posed by many, many older children and teens. Like their younger counterparts, they have been told that God is their best friend, and they know from personal experience that best friends willingly do many things for each other. Why, then, are prayers not answered, prayers that are not for "stupid stuff, but real problems," as one boy wrote. Adults don't like unanswered prayers any more than do children, but we understand that some things are even out of God's direct control. For example, when someone misuses free will and hurts another human being, it was not God's will but the will of a human being. Yet, there are many prayers for things over which God would seem to have control, such as the illness of a loved one. Why can't that person become healthy again? Or, as a ten-year-old said, "How come some people get miracles and others don't?" This is another one of those questions that can really only be answered by God. The rest of us have to settle for "I don't know." Because children often have strange ideas about why God does the things God does, it is *always* good to follow an "I don't know" with "What do you think?" in order for us to learn more about what the child thinks, and, if necessary, correct any erroneous ideas, such as people die because God hates them.

Jesus and His Experience on Earth

Five to Eight Years Old

How did Jesus walk on water? (6–7)
What was your childhood like? (8)

Nine to Twelve Years Old

> *Why did you pick Mary and Joseph? (9 G)*
> *If Mary had said no, who would you have picked? (9 G)*
> *When is Jesus coming back? (9–12)*
> *Is there only one Jesus? (9 B)*
> *Did it hurt on the cross? (9 G)*
> *Did you cry when Jesus died? (9 B)*
> *Why did you die for us when we're bad? (10 G)*
> *Why did you want to die? (10 B)*
> *Will Jesus return with a different face? (10 B)*
> *Did you feel sorry for yourself on the cross? (11 B)*
> *Why did you kill yourself for us? (12 B)*
> *What was it like to watch your son die? (12 B)*

Adolescents

> *Why were you willing to die? (13 B)*
> *How did you come back to life? (13 B)*
> *Was your life hard? (13 G)*
> *Were you really human? (14 G)*
> *Why didn't you stop Judas from leaving the Supper? (14 B)*
> *What was your experience as a teen? (15 G)*
> *Were you afraid when you were dying? (16 G)*

Since most, if not all, of the children were Christian, it is not surprising that children were curious about Jesus's life, especially his death and resurrection. Some of the questions are directed toward Jesus, and some are directed toward God the Father (i.e., "What was it like to watch your son die?"). We can certainly encourage children to speculate on the answers to their own questions, as we listen carefully, seek more information (when applicable), and correct any erroneous ideas that they might voice (e.g., "God the Father laughed when Jesus died.").

Jesus's death evokes particularly poignant questions. "Was Jesus in pain on the cross? Did he feel sadness?" Without being dramatic, we can respond that Jesus's death was a painful one and that as he was dying, he was probably very sad. To the question "Why did Jesus die?" we can respond that people who were jealous of Jesus killed him because they did not believe that he was good.

Likewise, because all the surveyed teens are Christian, there are naturally many questions about Christ, especially his life as a teen (about which the Gospels say nothing, except one episode when he was twelve years old) and his experience on the cross. Adolescents are both moved and bewildered by Jesus's crucifixion. They are old enough to understand the horror of Jesus's death, and they want to know how human Jesus was during it. "Were you afraid?" "Did you cry?" There are enough accounts of Jesus's crucifixion in the Gospels that, in responding to these questions, we can encourage the teen to read them, think about them, and discuss them with us and each other. This is especially true for Jesus's use of a line from Psalm 22 ("My God, my God, why have you forsaken me?"), which is recorded in the Gospel of Matthew, chapter 27, verse 46. Jesus himself used a verse from Scripture about feeling abandoned by God. Many young people resonate with this passage, precisely because they have—at times—felt abandoned by God. The wise adult listens as young people describe such times . . . without trying to negate the experience of the teen or sugar-coat it.

Which Religion Is Right?

Why do religions dislike other religions? (10 G)
Why do people have different names for you and beliefs about you?
  (11 B)
What religion are you? (11 G)
What's the correct religion? Which one do you like the best? (13 B)
Do you believe in another God? (14 B)
What do you want us to believe about you? (15 G)
Do you have a preference for how we worship you? (16 G)
Why do religions create discord with each other? (17 G)

At younger ages, many children do not even realize that there are a variety of religions, but as they become older, they learn about them in school and may even meet individuals of different faith traditions. By the time that children are ten to twelve years old, they are aware that there are many religions. In responding to questions about religions, we can note that people in different places often have different ways of thinking about God and even different names for God. Yet, Christians believe that there is only one God who loves each person.

To the question "Why do some religions dislike other religions?" we can answer that we don't know, because not everyone in a particular religion dislikes those in other religions; only certain people do that. For example, we can ask the child if he dislikes all people in another religion, to which he will probably say no. In using the child's own experiences, we can better address his concerns, but at the same time relay a truthful answer.

Teens are keenly aware that there are many religions, including at least one (Buddhism) that does not posit a personal God and several that believe there are many deities. Common adolescent questions in this area are "Why do we need so many religions if there is only one God?" and "Does God prefer a certain religion or religious ritual?" In responding to these questions, we can remind teens that different religious practices characterize different people and that God wants all people to love him. As long as people are striving to worship God in the ways that they genuinely believe to be best, their beliefs match their actions. Who can say whether God prefers a particular religious practice over another?

Teens also wonder why the various religions can't get along with each other. A helpful way to begin a discussion about this is to draw a parallel between children in a human family and children in God's family. In a human family, children often vie with one another to get their parents' attention and to be reassured that they are loved the most. Sometimes, children get attention by doing good things and sometimes by doing bad things. In God's family, adults (who are, after all, grown-up children) often seek to get God's attention—sometimes by doing good things and sometimes by doing bad things. In the end, they want to be assured of God's love and care.

God's Role in Evil

Five to Eight Years Old

> *Can you make people nice [stop fighting, stop wars]? (5–8)*
> *Did you make some people bad? (8 B)*
> *Why don't you kill the devil [Satan]? (8–10)*

Nine to Twelve Years Old

> *What do you do with bad people? (9 B)*

Do you love people who go to the devil? (9 G)
Why do you permit violence [death] if you love us? (10 G)
Why aren't you making the world better? (10 B)
How should the world be? (10 B)
Why did you let us sin? (10 B)
Why is there a devil? (11 G)
Why did you create bad [scary] things? (multiple)
If you love us, why did you make natural disasters? (11 B)
Why do you let people get hurt? (11 G)
How do you feel when someone sins? (11 G)
Are you happy with the way the world is? (11 G)
Why do you keep loving us when we're bad? (12 G)
Why did you make people who would turn against you? (multiple)
Why do some people hate you? (12 B)
Why don't you play a trick on the devil and kill him? (12 B)
Is this what you wanted the world to be? (12 G)

Adolescents

Why don't you stop cruelty? (13 G)
Why did you let the free will of one person cause 1,000,000 deaths in the Holocaust? (17 G)
What do you think of people dressing up like the devil on Halloween? (13)
Do you forgive murderers? (13 G)
Why did you let Adam and Eve eat the apple if you knew what was going to happen? (15 G)
Why did you create people with free will? (14 B)
Why do you bother with us? (14 G)
If you are in everyone, why are some people bad? (14 G)
What one thing about people would you most want to change? (14 G)
Why do you let bad things happen? (13 G)
Why is the world full of problems you won't solve? (13 B)
Do you forsake some people? (16 G)
Do you inflict pain, or does it just happen? (16 G)

Evil is troubling and frightening to children. They understand that God is perfect and good but cannot understand why the perfectly good God permits evil. These children (as would most adults) would eradicate evil if they could and would do anything to help those whom they love. Why won't God do the same? They would kill the devil. Why hasn't God done so? When children raise the question, "Why doesn't God kill off the devil?" we can respond that we don't know why the pervasiveness of evil has such a hold on our world and that evil cannot be killed as a human being can.

Why did God give human beings the power to do evil or to turn against God? These are difficult questions for adults as well. How much better the world would be if we would all use our free will for good purposes rather than for evil ones. Many of the questions posed by children have no answer, but we can be in solidarity with them in their distress over the evil that they see all around them. This lets children know that we are with them in their confusion and pain.

With their growing sophistication about the world, teens see evil all around them. How can a good God permit evil or suffering to exist? Where did the evil come from, if God made everything? In responding to questions such as the ones listed above, often the best that we can do is to say, "I don't know." The reality of evil is all around us. It cannot be denied. We adults don't know why it exists. And although much evil in the world is of human making, we, too, might struggle with the question "Was free will worth it?," especially if a loved one was harmed by someone else's free will. We can certainly commiserate with the frustration and bewilderment of teens as they grapple with these difficult issues, assuring them that we are in solidarity with them.

God's Role in Death

How do you know when someone dies? (8 G)
If you love us, why end the world? (9 B)
Why do you let tiny babies die? (9 G)
Why do you let death happen? (10 G)
Do you get upset when people cry, especially when loved ones die? (11 G)
How do you decide when someone dies? (11 B)
Do you make people die on purpose? (11 G)

Questions about God's role in death occur as children become older, as many younger children are not even aware that death is permanent.

"Why do we have to die?" In responding to these questions, we can note that death is just the end of this earthly life and the beginning of the next life. Although some people believe that God "kills" people at specific times, other people believe that individuals die when they are too sick or weak to live. In addition, some people die because other people kill them, something of which God would not approve. Although we cannot explain why some people die at the time and in the manner that they do, it is important to emphasize that God does not play games with people's lives, taking them at a whim. Just because we don't understand a situation doesn't necessarily mean that it is always wrong.

SAMPLE CONVERSATIONS

In the following examples, the goal is to encourage children to speak freely about their ideas about God and to offer any questions they might have. Obviously, a child's age, temperament, and native intelligence determines—at least in part—the direction that a conversation might go. Each hypothetical conversation is followed by the important points that it is meant to demonstrate.

Five to Eight Years Old

Child: I've been thinking about God a lot.

Adult: I did too when I was your age! What have you been thinking?

Child: I've been wondering what God looks like. Is God a giant?

Adult: Well, God is a spirit, so God doesn't have a body like we do.

Child: I think God is a BIG spirit!

Adult: You may be right.

Child: Does God ever get tired? Does God sleep?

Adult: Spirits don't get tired or sleepy.

Child: Is a spirit a ghost? I'm scared of ghosts!

Adult: No, people say a ghost is a human being who died. A spirit was not a human being.

Child: How did God become God?

Adult: God always existed. I know that sounds strange, but God always was and always will be. God is infinite. That means God has no limits.

Child: Wow! Do you think God would let me be God for a day?

Adult: Only God can be God. But if you were God, what would you do? [Discussion ensues.]

In this conversation, a young child is wondering about God's physical attributes, which is perfectly understandable at this age. The adult commiserates with the child by identifying with him in the child's very first question. She then answers all of the child's questions and poses a few of her own. This helps a young child to grow in understanding that it's hard to describe God who is a spirit and contributes to the relationship between child and adult.

* * *

Child: Do you think that God has ever been bad?

Adult: No, I don't. God is perfect. God is always good. Why do you ask?

Child: It's hard for me to be good all day.

Adult: Yes, I know. It was hard for me to be good all day when I was your age and even now.

Child: It's even hard for YOU to be good now?

Adult: It's hard for everyone to be good all day.

Child: If God is good, does he get mad at us when we're bad? Does he hate us?

Adult: God always loves us, even when we do bad things, but God might not like the bad things very much.

Child: Did God make bad people?

Adult: God didn't make bad people. God made people, and sometimes people do bad things.

Child: Do you think God cries when we do bad things?

Adult: I don't think God likes some of the things we do, but I don't know if God actually cries or not.

Child: I would cry if I were God. (Sighs) I think it must be hard being God.

Adult: I think so too. What do you think is the hardest part? [Discussion ensues.]

In this conversation, a young child has many questions about bad things: why are they here, and who does them? In a way, the child is asking about herself in terms of the "bad" things she does. The adult commiserates with the child's difficulty in being good all the time, answers questions, corrects misinformation, and moves the conversation along with questions of his own. In admitting that it's hard for him to be good all day, the adult shows empathy with the child's concern that she can't always be good and that God still loves her.

* * *

Child: Do you think God likes to play?

Adult: Hmmm, I never thought about that. Why do you ask?

Child: 'Cos I like playing and laughing with my friends, and I hope God likes to do that, too.

Adults: Well, God created us with the ability to laugh, make jokes, and play, so I'm sure God likes to see us having fun.

Child: Who would God play with?

Adult: What do you think?

Child: Angels?

Adult: You might be right! What game do you think God would like to play? [Discussion ensues.]

In this delightful conversation, a young child wonders how much God is like her: does God like to play and have fun as she does? The adult answers her questions, poses several of her own, engaging the child to imagine with whom God might share joy.

Nine to Twelve Years Old

Child: I'm mad at God.

Adult: Why?

Child: I asked God to make my best friend Emily's asthma better, but now she's in the hospital.

Adult: That's not good. I'm really sorry to hear that.

Child: Yeah, it's not like I was asking for something for myself. I was asking for her.

Adult: You were saying a nice prayer for Emily!

Child: Do you think God is mad at her?

Adult: No, I don't think God is angry at Emily. God doesn't make people sick at all, and God certainly wouldn't make people sick because he is angry at them.

Child: Could God be mad at me?

Adult: Why do you ask?

Child: Because if God's not mad at Emily, and God didn't answer my prayer for her, maybe it's my fault.

Adult: It's not your fault. God isn't angry at you. And even if he was, why would he take it out on your friend?

Child: I don't know. Maybe God is ignoring me or is too busy to hear my prayers.

Adult: God is never too busy for any of us because God loves each one of us very much. God would never ignore us.

Child: Then why is Emily getting sicker?

Adult: Sometimes people get sick, and we don't always know why. [Discussion ensues.]

In this conversation, an elementary school-age child is perplexed (and perhaps a bit angry) as to why God didn't answer his prayers for a friend. While the adult meets the child where he is in terms of his feelings (especially by saying she is sorry to hear of the friend's illness), the child wants to know if the reason for the unanswered prayer is something he (or the sick child) has done. The adult wisely corrects any misconceptions the child has, and as the discussion continues, explains why illness occurs.

* * *

Child: Do you think God likes the way the world turned out?

Adult: I've wondered about that myself. But why do you ask?

Child: Well, we learned that everything was perfect in the beginning, but it sure isn't perfect now. And human beings messed a lot of it up.

Adult: That's true.

Child: Do you think God gets mad at us when we mess up?

Adult: I think God understands that human beings are not perfect like he is. God knows that we will make mistakes.

Child: But how about if it's a huge mistake that hurts someone?

Adult: I think that God understands if we didn't mean to hurt someone by our mistake. I think that God is more concerned when we do things on purpose to hurt others.

Child: We say that God is in everybody. But if God is in everybody, how can they do bad things?

Adult: Because we have free will. That means that God lets us decide what we will do.

Child: I don't think free will is worth all the hurt it causes.

Adult: Well, I agree that some people don't use their free will for good things, but many people do. For example, you used your free will when you went door-to-door collecting money for the children hurt in the house fire.

Child: Yeah, I did.

Adult: How else can people use their free will for good purposes? [Discussion ensues.]

In this conversation, an elementary school-age child is troubled by the mess the world seems to be in and wonders if God is also upset by it. She asks a number of questions about it, especially focusing on people who hurt other people. The adult recognizes that this is a sophisticated conversation from this young person and answers her questions appropriately, agreeing and commiserating as needed. He also helps her to recall the good that she did and asks her to think creatively how people can do greater good.

* * *

Child: How does God keep everyone's prayers straight?

Adult: What do you mean?

Child: If a million people are praying at one time, how can God hear everybody? And if God can't hear everybody, they won't get what they want. And if God doesn't hear everyone right, someone might get something they didn't ask for!

Adult: Sounds like you've been thinking about this a lot.

Child: Yeah.

Adult: You know, computers keep a lot of things straight at one time; think of how many people use Google at one time.

Child: A gazillion!

Adult: I don't know if it's a gazillion, but it's a lot.

Child: But sometimes computers make mistakes.

Adult: But no one said a computer is perfect. Computers were made by human beings who are not perfect. God is perfect.

Child: I still don't understand how God keeps everything straight—like God's got a lot to do! I can't even remember when my friends' birthdays are!

Adult: God is awesome, that's for sure. I'm not sure that we'll ever understand how God's mind works.

In this conversation, an elementary school-age child cannot comprehend how God can be all-knowing and keep all of God's children's needs straight. The adult makes a connection to something with which this child is familiar (an internet search engine) and how it can handle a lot of requests at one time. The child wisely notes that computers can make mistakes, and the adult explains why, commiserating with the child that we won't ever be fully able to understand God's mind.

Adolescents

Adolescent: Isn't there just one God?

Adult: Yes.

Adolescent: Then why are there all these religions? They can't all be right.

Adult: Many religions developed long ago in certain cultures. The religious practices reflect the cultures. Regardless of one's religion, God loves each person as long as he or she tries to be the best person he or she can be.

Adolescent: Well, that's fine to say. But some religions hate people from other religions. That doesn't seem very holy to me.

Adult: Actually, it's really only some people in certain religions who don't like people in other religions. Most world religions preach tolerance and acceptance of each other.

Adolescent: I still don't get the conflict. Like, what's the purpose?

Adult: Well, I don't like all the conflict either. But, it's like a human family. In our family, the kids fight with each other, thinking that's the best way to get our attention. But we give them attention whether they fight or not. In God's family, some people fight with each other, thinking that's the best way to get God's attention and to show God that they're loyal to him. But God gives people attention, no matter what, because God loves each person.

Adolescent: I think God should write off some of his so-called children. They don't act like they love him.

Adult: Neither do we sometimes. I wouldn't want God to write me off on the days that I didn't do good things.

Adolescent: I don't mean little things. I mean big things.

Adult: Like what? [Discussion ensues.]

In this conversation, an adolescent is perplexed by the multiplicity of religions and the fact that they are often at odds with each other. The adult agrees and compares God's children's behaviors to that of children in a family, something with which an adolescent is very familiar. When the adolescent opines that God should write off some people because of their behavior, the adult counters that—at least on some days—that might be saying that God should write her off. As the adolescent tries to clarify what he means by "write-off" behavior, the adult encourages him to be specific. It will be in his ability to be specific that he will be able to understand why God cannot limit free will.

* * *

Adolescent: I think that God abandons some people.

Adult: Why do you say that?

Adolescent: I was watching a TV show about poverty in Africa. And it just seems like God forgot all about those poor people. Even the babies were dying of hunger and diseases that we got rid of in our country long ago.

Adult: It's very tragic, isn't it? That bothers me a lot, too.

Adolescent: Yeah, and if I were God, I'd make sure that they got food and medicine.

Adult: How would they get food and medicine?

Adolescent: People would bring them in.

Adult: That happens now.

Adolescent: But not enough! Some of the people's leaders take the stuff we send them and keep it all for themselves. That's evil.

Adult: I agree. But how is that God's fault?

Adolescent: God should kill those people instead of the babies.

Adult: God doesn't kill anybody—not people who do bad thing and not little babies.

Adolescent: But God lets it all happen.

Adult: Why might God let these things happen? [Discussion ensues.]

In this conversation, an adolescent is disturbed by the suffering in the world after she has seen a TV program. She rails against the unfairness of it all, and the adult commiserates, acknowledging the tragedy. The teen attempts to blame God for it all, and the adult asks the adolescent to consider her statement, pointing out that human beings play an important role in the tragedy. When the adolescent is frustrated that God doesn't do more, especially to people who make the tragedy worse, the adult encourages the adolescent to consider why God permits a tragedy, thereby enlarging her understanding of the many tragedies in the world.

* * *

Adolescent: I just don't get how God could have existed always. Like everything began sometime. Science tells us that.

Adult: It is certainly hard for human beings to understand that because we think in terms of time.

Adolescent: OK, I can see how something could go on forever, but I don't understand it when we say there's no beginning.

Adult: It doesn't seem to make sense, does it? But to say God had a beginning would mean that something or someone had to bring God into existence, right?

Adolescent: Yeah.

Adult: So who or what brought God into existence?

Adolescent: I don't know.

Adult: Neither do I. But you see what I'm saying? If there was a some-thing or someone that brought God into existence, how did that thing or being come into existence?

Adolescent: Did God create himself?

Adult: How could that happen? If there was nothing and no God, how could God then come into existence?

Adolescent: This makes my brain hurt!

Adult: Mine, too! But it's not a question that we can really find a logical answer to, which is why we say God always existed.

In this conversation, the adolescent, appealing to science, questions how God could have existed always. The adult commiserates with the question and furthers the interaction by asking the adolescent how the first of anything or any being came into being. When the adolescent expresses complete confusion, the adult joins him in this and draws the conclusion that religions have come up with. This type of interchange helps adolescents grapple with questions that have no easy answers, encouraging them to think deeply about what we are told . . . from any source.

Chapter 3

Children's Questions about Themselves

Five to Eight Years Old

Why are people so mean [nasty, bad] to me [ignore me]? Why can't people be nice to me? (5–8)

Nine to Twelve Years Old

Am I [have I been] bad? Was I good today? (9–12)
Will you help me? (9–12)
Why don't you answer prayers from me? (9–12)
Why must life be hard [unfair]? (9–11)
Will you keep me safe [always help me]? (11)

Thirteen Years and Older

What sin have I done the most? (13 B)
What happens to me if I break one of your laws? (13 B)
Why? (13 B)
How can I improve? How can I be better? (13 G)

INTRODUCTION

Like most human beings of all ages, children and teens have questions about themselves, but young people's questions differ from those of older people. After all, once we are adults, we pretty much know what our interests are, where our strengths lie, and what form our growing edges take. Children and teens don't have enough experience with themselves to know that information.

Try to think back to when you were a child or teen; didn't you have many questions about how your life would turn out? For children and teens, the future is a large mystery. What will they be when they grow up? Will they get married and have children? Will they be famous, rich, or brilliant? Since God knows the future in a way that their parents can't, it makes sense for them to address such questions to God.

But children and teens have questions about the here and now as well, and perhaps these are the more profound questions. When a child asks God why no one wants him on the team, and when another child asks God why people are so mean to her, such questions reveal much about a child's state of mind and his or her fears and feelings of worth. It is at these times that adults must listen *very* carefully to what a child or teen has to say without interruption or judgment, and without trivializing what is being said. For example, although *we* might know—from our own experiences—that friendships and romances don't last forever, children and teens are not so aware. If we dismiss their concerns with "You'll get more friends" or "You can't be in love at your age," young people will feel that we don't understand them or—worse yet—are making fun of them. As another example, children and teens don't understand why they struggle in school, especially if others in their class or siblings do not; they don't yet understand that all of us have gifts and growing edges. They see what others can do and want to do the same as well . . . or better. And since God made them, they may wonder why God didn't make them smarter, prettier, more athletic, and so on. They wonder if God truly loves them just the way they are. Thus, it does no good when questions about their abilities arise for adults to "toughen them up" by berating them for not studying harder or practicing more. The goal is to listen to what is being said before speaking, and even then, to truly ponder what should be said in response to what was said (and what was not said).

WHAT THE SURVEYS REVEAL

Children's questions about themselves came in second in frequency only to questions about God. There are so many things that children want to know about themselves, and, in many cases, only God can answer these questions. From the charming ("Can I have my teeth back?") to the poignant ("Why can't friendship last forever?"), children's and teens' questions reveal the nitty-gritty of their daily lives. Try to recall some of your own questions about yourself and your life when you were a child; how would you answer that child now with the knowledge and experience you now have?

Because there are so many questions in this category, topics will be discussed in sub-categories.

QUESTIONS

Wishes

Five to Eight Years Old

> *Can I have a baby sister [brother]? (5–8)*
> *Can I have a [dog, puppy, etc.]? (5–8)*
> *Can you make me funny, [smart, happy]? (6–8)*
> *Will you help me do better in school [write neat]? (6–8)*
> *Will you help me to be nicer [good, listen to you better]? (7–8)*
> *Can you make my bad dreams stop? (5 B)*
> *Can I have just one friend? (5 G)*
> *Can I live forever? (6 G)*
> *Can I be an angel? (6 G)*
> *Can I see my angel? (6 G)*
> *Can you make me good? (8 B)*
> *Can I get well one day? (8 G)*

At young ages, the questions that many children ask concern whether they can have something—a new sibling, a puppy, a toy, etc. This is completely normal. Since God possesses everything, children believe that God can supply their desires as well as their needs. This is best illustrated by the child who said, "Why can't I have everything I want?"

In responding to such questions, it is helpful to explain the difference between something a child needs (e.g., food) and something a child wants (e.g., candy).

This type of question is much less likely to be offered by older children and teens, and when they offer it, it is less about having something and more about being able to do something (e.g., "Can I be a better person?"). For example, older children requested the ability to fly, good grades, a picture of God or a sign that God is real, the ability to perform a miracle, living forever, some of God's power, and the chance to be God for a week. Since God can do anything, the children believe that all these gifts are God's to give, and they would like a bit of the action! On the other hand, many of the questions are like those asked by their younger counterparts, questions that are much more serious or profound.

The Future

Five to Eight Years Old

> *How long will I live? (5–8)*
> *What will I be when I grow up? (6–8)*
> *What will I look like when I get older? (6 B)*
> *Will I live with you forever one day? (8 G)*
> *How many good deeds must I do to become a saint? (8 B)*
> *Who will I marry? How many children will I have? (8 G)*
> *Are you going to make me die someday? (8 B)*
> *If I die, can I come back to life? (8 B)*
> *What's it like to die? (8 G)*

Nine to Twelve Years Old

> *Why am I here? What's my purpose? (9–12)*
> *What will I be when I grow up? (9–12)*
> *Will I marry? Will I have children? (9–12)*
> *What's my future? What will I become? Will I be rich? Will my life turn out OK? (9–12)*
> *When will I die? How? (9–12)*
> *Will I become a famous saint? (9 G)*
> *Will I get good grades? (9 G)*

Will I ever be good at anything? (12 B)
Will I get taller? (12 B)
Am I going to be a big sinner? (12 B)
Will I ever have grandchildren? (12 B)

Adolescents

> *What's my future? What will I become? Will I be rich? Will I get married? Will my life turn out OK? (13–16)*

Young children wonder what they will be when they grow up, and many children tell God what they hope to be (e.g., sports star, music star). They are also interested in whom they will marry and how many children they will have. Naturally, there are no certain answers to these questions, but we can encourage children to dream a bit about what they might be . . . and how they might begin now to achieve their goal. Also in this category are very common questions about how long they will live. Children wonder what it's like to die, whether they will be with God forever, and whether they will be able to come back to life, a common hope for younger children, since they are not fully cognizant of the finality of death until about age 7 or 8. Unless there is reason to believe otherwise (e.g., the presence of a terminal illness), children can be reassured that they will probably live long lives, and that God wants them to be with him forever after they die.

Older children are also quite interested in what they will become when they grow up, whether that will be a sports star or a saint. They want to know if they will marry and have children, if they will be successful or rich, and if, in general, their lives will turn out well. Having a better understanding of growing up than do younger children, these older children often plan a strategy for how they will achieve their goals. When discussing these issues with children, we can encourage them to be everything that they can be. No one can be all things; that is true for adults as well as children, but we can all be the best that we can be. That takes attention on our part. Sharing your own thoughts about what you hoped to be at various ages in childhood in adolescence will help the young person to see that such questions (and the dreams associated with them) are perfectly normal.

Older children wonder how long they will live; this is phrased either as a general question or as a specific one, such as, "Can I live to be

399?" Naturally, these children also wonder about death—what it is like, when and how it will come for them, whether it might be possible to come back after death (i.e., is reincarnation real?). As one ten-year-old said, "Was I here before?" They are concerned that no one will remember them when they die; they are also concerned that they won't remember others, especially family members, once they die. We can reassure children that, although we don't know what death is like precisely, we do know that they probably will not die soon and that they will have more knowledge after death, not less. Where they will end up after they die is another area of concern. They wonder if they will go to heaven (or as one ten-year-old asked, "Am I going up or down?"); Catholic children might also wonder if they will be in purgatory and for how long. (Purgatory is an intermediate state after death when one is purged of any sins and becomes purified.) We can assure children that God wants all of us to be with him forever.

Abilities and Deficiencies

Five to Eight Years Old

> *Why can't I walk like other kids? (5 G)*
> *Why can't I live with my mom and dad? (5 B)*
> *Why can't I have everything I want? (5 B)*
> *Why do I sin? (8 G)*
> *Will you always forgive me? (8 G)*
> *Why can't I see you? (8 G)*
> *Why am I so little [stupid, etc.]? (multiple)*
> *Why do I struggle with things at home and in school? (8 B)*
> *Why do I have to wear glasses? (8 B)*
> *When I run, why do you pick me to fall and hurt myself? (8 G)*

Nine to Twelve Years Old

> *Why am I so poor? (9 G)*
> *Why am I bad? (9 B)*
> *Why am I so short? (10 G)*
> *Why can't I be smarter? (11 G)*
> *Why did you make me as I am? (11 B)*

Adolescents

> *Have I been good enough? (13 B)*
> *Why did you make me like I am? (13 B)*
> *Why did you make me a boy? (13 B)*
> *Why did you create me if I might not be successful? (13 G)*
> *What am I really like? (14 G)*

Young children have many questions about why they are the way they are—why so short, so dumb, so ugly, and so on. Closely related to this question is an appeal to God to make them something better—good, smarter, prettier, taller, nicer, funnier, or more popular. In answering these questions, we can emphasize that we (and God) love a child just the way he or she is, but that we can always ask God to be better persons because God wants us to be the best that we can be. Especially touching is the question of an eight-year-old boy: "Why do I struggle with things at home and at school?" The sensitive adult who responds to such a question would not automatically say, "You're fine just the way you are," or, "Don't think that way." Instead, the adult would gently probe the child to find out with what he or she is struggling *even if the adult thinks he or she already knows the answer*. In meeting children and teens where they are, it is important to know what they are thinking before offering reassurance that might seem to be superficial.

Young children ask God why they cry so much, fight with their siblings or friends, or sin. In Romans 7:15, St. Paul wrote, "I do not understand what I do. For what I want to do I do not do, but what I hate I do." Like St. Paul, young children don't always understand the wrong things that they do (and why they did them), especially when they feel bad about doing them afterward. We can remind children of St. Paul's words, noting that even a great saint had the same difficulties. When children ask why they cry so much, a gentle exploration of what is making them so sad is in order. If it is something about which we can reassure them, we should do so. If not, we should get them help. No child should cry a great deal. Especially poignant is the question of an eight-year-old boy: "How many pieces of hurt are on my heart?"

Like their younger counterparts, older children are also not always satisfied with who they are or how they look. So, they wonder about why they are short, poor, or bad. They question why they can't be smarter or more popular. A common question of this age group was one asking God why life was hard or unfair, especially regarding their own abilities. "Will I ever be good at anything?" cried a twelve-year-old boy. "Am I good enough?" asked an eleven-year-old. Another child raised the moving question: "Do you [i.e., God] think I'm stupid?"

In responding to these questions, we can assure children that they are, indeed, good enough. They are uniquely who they are, and it is good. We can remind children that they are not bad, although they might do bad things. We can assure them of God's love and assistance, and we can remind them that God does not think they are stupid, even when they do stupid things, things which God understands and forgives. God is always there for them—to help them, to care for them. They do well to ask God, "What do you want me to do today?" knowing that God will never lead them astray.

Some children wonder if they have been bad (or good) on a particular day and whether God will help them to do better. Many times, for a particular day, they wonder why they and their siblings fought, why they misbehaved in school, or why they evoked parental anger or disappointment. In responding to that concern, we can note that God never leaves any of us, even when we sin or do things that we later regret. We can always tell God that we are sorry and then apologize to the person whom we offended in some way.

Teens often wonder whether they are good enough and whether they are living up to their potential. They ask if they are doing what they are supposed to be doing at this point in their lives. They also wonder if there is a plan established for their lives or if things just happen. Many ask God for ways that they can improve, while others berate themselves for their shortcomings. We can listen attentively, reminding them that it is never too late to improve but also that God loves them as they are and wants the best for them. God wants them to be all that they can be. Then, we can explore with teens how *they* think that they can improve and the ways that they might accomplish that.

Some older children and teens ask positive questions: "What do you like the most about me?" "What do you think of when you think of me?" "Why did you make me, me?" "How am I special?" Such questions indicate a child who has a robust relationship with God, confident in God's love for them. They are to be celebrated!

Relationship with Loved Ones

Five to Eight Years Old

> *Do I belong to my family? (6 G)*
> *Why do my sister and I fight? (7 B)*
> *Will my mom and dad see my children? (7 G)*
> *Do my brothers and sisters like me? (8 B)*

Nine to Twelve Years Old

> *Can I see my real mom one day? (9 B)*
> *Why does my sister [brother, mom, dad] fight so much? (9–12)*
> *Do my parents [does my dad, mom] really love me? (9 G)*
> *Can my mom, dad, and me live together again? (9 G)*
> *Will I ever see my brother again? (9 G)*
> *When is it OK to hit my sister? (10 B)*
> *Does my mother really love me? (10 G)*
> *Will I ever have a family that doesn't make me feel bad? (12 G)*
> *Why does my brother hate me? (12 G)*
> *Will my folks adopt me? (12 B)*
> *Why did my real parents put me up for adoption? (12 G)*

Young children wonder if family members love them and want them. They wonder why they can't see absent family members more often ("Why doesn't my real mom visit me?") and whether they really belong to their family. They worry about whether their parents will be around when they grow up, a concern that might be very legitimate when parents are ill. In responding to these questions, we can usually assure them of parental and sibling love but remind them that no one is perfect and that sometimes people don't show their love. In the cases when parental love is truly absent, we can commiserate with a child's pain and assure her of our care.

Older children have many of the same concerns as do younger children regarding family members. They worry if their parents or siblings really love them; if they love them, why is there fighting in their house? They ask why they can't have families that don't make them feel bad or families that can live together happily. Some children wonder why their real parents left them and whether they still think or care about them. Other children wonder why they were placed for adoption, and if their current family will love them enough to adopt them. Obviously, these are complex questions. In responding to such concerns, we can reassure children that their parents and siblings do love them (unless we have glaring evidence to the contrary), and that even people who love others hurt them sometimes. We can ask if they have ever hurt someone whom they liked or loved. Because most children will say yes, we can then remind them that no one is perfect, except God. We can commiserate when a child lives in a condition that makes him feel bad and reassure him or her of God's constant care. If we believe that a child's situation warrants intervention, we can seek that on his behalf.

Being abandoned by a parent is a very difficult reality with which a child must come to terms. In answering questions about abandonment or adoption, we must emphasize how much the child is loved by his or her current family. We need to listen well to let the child express all the fears and anger he or she might have. Trying to "talk a child out of" any fears or negative feelings is usually unsuccessful. The most successful way to alleviate a child's (or anyone's, for that matter) fears, doubts, or negative emotions is to demonstrate love toward him or her. Love often means accepting loved ones as they are, while always trying to encourage growth and more positive emotions.

Personal Illness and Conditions

Will my asthma get better one day? (6 G)
Why does my head hurt all the time? (6 B)
Why do I cry so much? (6 G)
Why do I get sick so much? (9 B)
Will my thyroid get better? (9 G)
Will my asthma go away? (11 G)
Will I ever get cancer? (11 B)
Why do I always get badly injured? (11 B)
Why do I have diabetes? (12 G)

Children wonder whether their asthma, headaches, diabetes, and other illnesses will ever get better. It is difficult to be young and ill; it is so unfair. When children of this age aren't like their peers and can't do what they do, their self-esteem falters. Why did God make them like this? Especially poignant is the eight-year-old girl who asked, "When I run, why do you pick me to fall and hurt myself?" In responding to this question, we can assure children that although their suffering is very real, God does not make them suffer or rejoice in their suffering. God is always with them and on their side. In addition, we are there with them and accept them as they are, no matter what the other kids do.

Finally, we can remind them that the children who are giving them a hard time simply don't understand what they are going through. To help them better understand this, we can ask whether *they* did not understand what someone was going through at some point. Because many children will respond affirmatively to such a question, we can then ask if the lack of understanding was intentional or accidental (i.e., the child didn't know any better). Most children will respond that they didn't do it on purpose. We can draw a comparison to how they are being treated in the present, allowing for the fact that at least some children whom they perceive as not being nice do not understand their situation.

No one wants to be ill or disabled, and most very much want to fit in with their peers. That makes it doubly difficult for children to reconcile a loving God who can do everything with their situations and doesn't (in their minds) do anything. Their questions reveal their frustration and fears: "Why do I get sick so much?"; "Will my thyroid get better?"; "Will my asthma go away?"; "Why do I always get hurt?"; "Why do I have diabetes?"; and "Will I ever get cancer?" Because it is natural to think that children should be healthy, ill children have some very real concerns about their health. In addition, some children have had relatives who have been very ill and worry that they, too, would get the disease; this was the case with the child who asked if he would ever get cancer like his dad. Although we do not want to reassure a child that he or she will get better if, in fact, that is not likely to be the case, oftentimes, conditions in childhood do improve over time, so some careful reassurance can be offered. As with other concerns, we can reassure children of God's constant care and love. We can also assure them of our own care.

Yet, children frequently ask a difficult question—"Why don't you [God] answer my prayers?" For many children, their prayers—especially in the areas of their own illnesses or those of loved ones—are profound, as they seek healing for themselves and for loved ones. So, if God is their best friend and they are asking for something important, why does God not answer the prayer? The difficulty of unanswered prayers strikes this age group particularly hard, since they understand the meaning of friendship in their own lives. They often go out of their way for their own friends. In addressing this question, we can commiserate with them, because it is likely that all of our prayers have not been answered. Hence, we understand the children's disappointment and maybe even annoyance at God. Yet, we must remind children that we don't have all the facts of a situation. We can explain that two people might see a situation completely differently. If they each pray for the outcome that they desire, only one will be happy, while the other will believe that prayers have been unanswered. In such a case, who is right? Things might not be as they seem on the surface.

Current Life

Why do I cry a lot? (9 G)
Why does living hurt? (12 G)
Why am I punished for something I didn't do? (14 G)
Do you love me as much as when I was little? (14 G)
Why is my life so painful? (15 G)
Why am I who I am? (15 G)
Why did my parents have me at such an old age? (15 G)
Am I where you want me to be at this point in my life? (15 G)
Why am I slow? (15 G)
Why did the hard things in my life have to happen to me? (16 G)
Do I deserve the life I have? (16 G)

Like younger children, teens wonder why their lives are hard and painful, and why it seems like they are being punished for something. If truth be told, many of us felt that way when we were young and feel the same way now, at least occasionally, and many teens have lives that are harder than those of many adults. In responding to this question, we can commiserate with teens, listening carefully when they describe the hard parts of their lives. We can reassure them of our own care and concern and that they can always speak to us. Finally, we can assure them that God is with them, even though it might not always seem that way, and that the kindness of other people is one of God's ways to help them.

If it seems like a child or teen is in need of some type of intervention, that should be sought as soon as possible.

God's Relationship with the Child or Teen

Do you love me? (5–8)
Do you think I'm bad [mean]? (5–8)
Do you really love me? (7 G)
Do you always hear me? (7 B)
Why don't you talk out loud to me? (7 G)
Will you always be with me? (8 G)
Do you always listen to my prayers? Always? (8 G)
Can I be a saint? (9 G)
Am I doing OK so far? (11 B)
Do you approve of me? (12 G)
Do you always know what I'm doing? (13 G)
Are you disappointed in me? (16 G)

Both younger and older children ask God whether he will always for-give them, help them, love them, and want them. It is scary to think that God will not always love or forgive! About this, they can be reassured that God is on their side, always hears their prayers, and is always with them, even though they cannot see God. They cannot see God because God is a spirit, and spirits don't have bodies as we do. Many children are interested in whether they will become saints and live with God forever in heaven. We can respond that God wants us all to be saints (in the broad sense of that word), to be more like him, and live with him forever. We should also point out that even saints are not perfect—they make mistakes or hurt others. But they kept trying to do better, a mes-sage we can share (repeatedly) with children and teens.

Teens wonder if God is disappointed in the way they are living their lives or angry at them because of the wrongs that they do. As mentioned above, they wonder if God loves them as they are (or as a fourteen-year-old girl noted, "Do you love me as much as when I was little?") and why. Teens know that they disobey God and break his laws; one thirteen-year-old was interested in which sin he had done the most. They wonder what might happen to them because of these transgres-sions. In hearing such concerns, we can remind these young people that God is love and is always eager to forgive, no matter what we do. God knows what we do (or don't do) and why, even before we are aware of our own motives and continues to sustain us.

SAMPLE CONVERSATIONS

In the following examples, the goal is to encourage children to speak freely about their questions about themselves. Obviously, a child's age, temperament, and native intelligence determine—at least in part—the direction that a conversation might go. In some cases, reassurance is all that is needed. Each hypothetical conversation is followed by the important points that it is meant to demonstrate.

Five to Eight Years Old

Child: Why can't people be nice to me?

Adult: Who is not nice to you?

Child: Kids in my class. They laugh at me because I don't always read right.

Adult: That's not very nice. There are probably things that you can do that they can't.

Child: I'm better at running than everybody else. But you know what? One of the kids said that God made me dumb.

Adult: That is not kind. It's also not true.

Child: But if God made me, and if I'm not smart, then God made me like that.

Adult: God did make you, but God doesn't make people dumb or smart. God gives people gifts, and it's up to them to use those gifts so that they will be the best that they can be.

Child: What are my gifts?

Adult: You're friendly and forgiving. And you are smart in many, many ways.

Child: How am I smart?

Adult: You're good at arithmetic. And you're good at drawing.

Child: I am. That's really cool.

Adult: Let's think of some other gifts you have. [Discussion ensues.]

In this conversation, a young child is concerned that other children are not nice and make fun of him, saying that he's dumb, and that God (who made everyone) must have made him that way. The adult refutes that allegation, clearly identifying it as wrong. He takes the child's side, naming several of the child's gifts. This encourages bonding between an adult and a child. The adult then asks him to think of other gifts he has, furthering the conversation and—more importantly—the child's understanding of himself.

* * *

Child: How long do you think that I'll live?

Adult: Until you're very old. Why do you ask?

Child: We were talking in class about heaven, and everybody said that they wanted to go to heaven, but I said that I don't want to go yet!

Adult: I don't want you to go yet either! But I don't think that you have anything to worry about.

Child: I asked God to let me live a lot longer.

Adult: And I'm sure that God liked that prayer, because God wants health for everyone.

Child: Doesn't God make us die?

Adult: No, dying is the end of life. God doesn't make us die.

Child: Then why can't we live forever?

Adult: Well, we do live forever with God in heaven after we die.

Child: I mean here on earth.

Adult: No living thing lives forever. Plants die. Animals die. People die.

Child: I don't like it.

Adult: I can understand that. I don't like it either.

Child: But why can't we come back to life again?

Adult: Because we only have one earthly life, and when it's over, it's over.

Child: I want to come back when I die.

Adult: As what?

Child: As a kid.

Adult: That would be nice, wouldn't it?

In this conversation, the young child is reporting a classroom discussion. Being literal, she is concerned that if she says she wants to go to heaven, she might have to go right now! The adult reassures her, but the child is confused when the adult notes that God wants health for everyone, because the child thinks God makes people die. The adult commiserates with the child's dislike of dying but notes it's part of life. When the child wonders if she can come back, the adult doesn't argue but—instead—asks her what she would like to come back as, fully engaging with the child's dreams.

* * *

Child: Does God know what I'm thinking before I tell God?

Adult: God knows everything; we don't have to say it.

Child: Oooh, that's scary!

Adult: How come?

Child: Because sometimes I don't think very nice thoughts about people.

Adult: I think that's true of almost everybody, at least sometime.

Child: If God knows what I'm thinking, can God force me to do something I don't want to do?

Adult: No, that's not how God works. God gave us free will. Do you know what that is?

Child: No.

Adult: It means that God gave us the ability to make decisions and choices.

Child: Suppose I pick the wrong thing?

Adult: Unfortunately, that happens to everybody—at least sometimes. Did you ever think that you picked the wrong thing? [Discussion ensues.]

In this conversation, a young child is a bit frightened by the notion that God knows our thoughts . . . because sometimes his thoughts aren't very nice, with which the adult rightly commiserates! The child then wonders if God could force him to do something that he didn't want to do (a scary thought), which the adult refutes but uses the moment as an opportunity to say something about free will—apparently a new concept for this child—and to open a conversation about choices and picking the wrong thing. Both of these topics can expand a young child's moral capacity.

Nine to Twelve Years Old

Child: Why doesn't God answer prayers?

Adult: Is this about one of your prayers?

Child: Yeah.

Adult: What did you pray for?

Child: I prayed that my grandmother wouldn't die, but she died of cancer last week.

Adult: I'm sorry; I bet you miss her.

Child: A lot.

Adult: And you prayed for her to live, and you don't understand why God didn't answer your prayers.

Child: Yeah, it was a good prayer, too. I wasn't asking for junk.

Adult: It's very hard when someone you love dies.

Child: Maybe God is mad at me.

Adult: I don't think so. What did you do that was so wrong that he would let your grandmother die just because he was mad at you?

Child: I don't know. Maybe he's testing me. I heard that once in church.

Adult: Testing you? To see if you do what?

Child: If I get mad at him.

Adult: Are you mad at God?

Child: A little. I miss my grandma.

Adult: I'm sure you do.

Child: Maybe he didn't hear my prayers or he's too busy for me.

Adult: God knows everything, so I'm sure he heard your prayers. And God is never too busy for one of his children.

Child: Then why didn't he answer my prayer? Why didn't he let grandma live?

Adult: I don't know, but I'll bet that your grandma is with God right now.

Child: Really? That would be neat. But I still miss her.

Adult: How could you do something that honors your grandmother? What would it be? [Discussion ensues.]

Unanswered prayers are hard for any of us to understand, especially when they are for people we love. In this conversation, an elementary school-age child is upset that his prayers for his grandmother didn't keep her alive. Note that the adult is thoroughly empathetic here and engages this child fully when he gives various reasons for why the prayer was not answered. When the child admits he might be "a little" mad at God, the adult doesn't argue or reprimand him. Instead, the adult acknowledges that she doesn't know why his grandmother had to die at this point and encourages the child to do something that would honor his grandmother, keeping her memory alive, something to which a child who misses a loved one a great deal would be very open.

* * *

Child: I'm tired of being sick.

Adult: I know you are.

Child: None of my friends are sick. I feel so weird.

Adult: It's hard for you to know that you can't do things that your friends can do.

Child: Yeah, and I have to take medicine all the time so I won't get sicker.

Adult: And the medicine helps you to stay healthy, right?

Child: I guess so. I just want to be like everyone else.

Adult: I don't blame you.

Child: You think God is happy that I'm sick?

Adult: I don't think that God wants any of us to be sick. Remember how Jesus went around and cured the sick people he met?

Child: I wish Jesus would do that for me.

Adult: I do, too.

Child: If God can do anything, why doesn't God make me well?

Adult: I don't know. What do you think?

Child: At first, I thought it was because I did something bad. But I haven't been that bad.

Adult: I don't think that you're sick because you were bad.

Child: So I don't know why I'm sick, but I'd like to get better. I pray—hard—but I don't get better.

Adult: Praying is good, even though we don't always get what we want when we pray. Praying is talking to God. It's good to talk to God at all times, but especially when we're sick or in trouble.

Child: I wish God would answer my prayer.

Adult: I do, too. (pause) Would you like us to pray right now?

Being ill is like a punishment: you can't do what you want when you want to do it. In this conversation, an elementary school-age child with a chronic condition (asthma) just wants to be like everyone else and doesn't want to have to take medicine. The adult emphasizes fully and is honest that he doesn't know why she isn't healed of her asthma, all the while underscoring that it is not because the child has been bad or unworthy. With regard to her unanswered prayer about getting well, the wise adult consistently takes the child's side and reads the child's demeanor, which is the purpose of the pause. Would the child like to pray, or does that seem out of the question? The adult lets the child take the lead.

* * *

Child: I don't like being adopted.

Adult: Tell me more.

Child: I mean, why didn't my real parents love me enough to keep me?

Adult: I don't know if your parents didn't love you, but they couldn't take care of you and wanted the best for you. That's why they permitted you to be adopted. We are so happy that you are part of our family now, because we want you and love you . . . a lot.

Child: I kinda know that, but our teacher said that no love is better than a mother's love, but my mother didn't love me enough to keep me.

Adult: You are my child, and I am your mother. I love you.

Child: Maybe, someday if I'm bad, you won't want to keep me too?

Adult: Never.

Child: Why did God give me a mother who didn't want me?

Adult: God wants all mothers to love their children, just as I love you. But sometimes human beings have problems that make it hard for them to love as they should.

Child: Does God think I'm not as good as some kids because my mother didn't want me?

Adult: What gave you that idea?

Child: It's something I've been thinking about. Maybe God doesn't want me . . .

Adult: Let's talk some more. [Discussion ensues.]

In this conversation, an adopted elementary school-age child is concluding that she needed to be adopted because her birth parents didn't want her. Whether that is true or not, the adoptive parent answers honestly about the birth parents' motives but emphasizes that she is delighted that the child is now part of the family and that she (the adult) is now her mother, and the child is now hers. When the child fears that the adoptive mother might one day abandon her (a very common fear), she is reassured that this will not be the case. As the child wonders about God's opinion of her, the real issue surfaces: maybe God doesn't want her either. This response requires a much longer conversation and probably multiple ones.

Adolescents

Adolescent: Do you think that God loves me as much as he did when I was younger?

Adult: Of course. God's love is not based on a person's age. Why do you ask?

Adolescent: Well, when a person gets older, they sin more. Little kids don't sin. So I thought that God likes little kids better than older people.

Adult: God loves all of us, even when we sin.

Adolescent: It's hard realizing that you're not as good as you thought you were.

Adult: Are you talking about yourself?

Adolescent: Yeah, I do a lot of stuff that I wish I didn't do. Sometimes, I wonder if God gets tired of all my sins.

Adult: God never gets tired of you. All of us do things we wish we didn't do and don't do things we should have done. I know I do. But God loves us all and wants to help us to be the best that we can be.

Adolescent: I pray for that every day. So why doesn't it happen?

Adult: I don't know. I pray that I am better each day, but it doesn't always happen for me either.

Adolescent: Really? I thought it would be different when I grew up.

Adult: Not really. We human beings are a complicated bunch. Even St. Paul wondered why he did the things he didn't want to do and didn't do the things he wanted to do. Would you like to see the part in the Bible where he says that?

Adolescent: Yeah.

Adult: [Shows the teen the passage and continues the discussion.]

Adolescents are beginning to realize that they were more innocent when they were younger. In this conversation, an adolescent wonders if God liked him better when he was more innocent. The adult shows great empathy by noting he also does things that he shouldn't do and by sharing that his prayers to get better aren't always answered in the way he'd like (in answer to the adolescent's comment about prayers). To further the conversation, he mentions that even great saints have the same issues and asks if the teen would like to see a passage from St. Paul illustrating that; this can be a springboard to further discussions.

* * *

Adolescent: Why does God let my life be so crummy?

Adult: What do you mean?

Adolescent: First, my dad lost his job. Then, my girlfriend broke up with me. And I just failed my Algebra final.

Adult: This is a really tough time for you.

Adolescent: Yeah, it is.

Adult: How do you feel about God?

Adolescent: Like he let me down.

Adult: That can be a rough feeling. Do you think that God is giving you the crummy life?

Adolescent: No, I don't believe God does that. I mean, I failed my exam because I didn't study. My girlfriend likes someone else. My father's job was cut because of the economy. God didn't do any of that. But God let it happen.

Adult: What was God supposed to do?

Adolescent: I don't know.

Adult: Even though everything that has happened was due to human free will, it still feels like God could have done something.

Adolescent: Yeah.

Adult: Well, human free will is a great gift that God didn't give to us and then take back. Just like you couldn't stop your girlfriend from liking another guy, God can't stop you from not studying.

Adolescent: He can't, or he won't?

Adult: He won't because he honors us too much as free creatures.

Adolescent: I'm not sure that free will is worth it. It causes too much sadness.

Adult: It sure seems like it sometimes, doesn't it? But human free will permits us to do wonderful things, too. It isn't all bad stuff.

Adolescent: Yeah, but lately, I've been thinking about the bad stuff that people do. It makes me sad; it really does.

Adult: Me, too.

In this conversation, the adolescent seems to be blaming God for all the things that are going wrong in his life, although he clearly acknowledges that God isn't causing these bad things, nor is God entirely to blame. As the adult commiserates and asks clarifying questions, she reminds the teen of free will, with the teen countering that free will might not be worth all the pain it causes. The adult agrees but points out the converse side of free will—allowing us to do the good and not just the bad. Throughout, the adult is thoroughly empathetic with the teen's thoughts about his life, without being patronizing.

* * *

Adolescent: I hate that I never feel well.

Adult: I don't like it either.

Adolescent: Why did God give me diabetes?

Adult: God didn't "give it" to you. You probably have it because I have it, and it's passed down in the genes.

Adolescent: But you're not as sick with yours as I am with mine.

Adult: I know, and I'm sorry you're having such a rough time with it.

Adolescent: No one wants to be my friend because if we go somewhere and I have to watch what I eat. I'm not worth being a friend to.

Adult: I disagree; I think you're worth it.

Adolescent: Does God want me to never get married?

Adult: Whoa . . . I thought we were talking about diabetes.

Adolescent: Well, maybe no one will want me if I'm such a pain to be around. Maybe this is God's way of making me single all my life.

Adult: I don't think so. After all, I have diabetes, and I got married.

Adolescent: But you're not as sick as I've been. Maybe God is trying to tell me that I'll die young.

Adult: Do you think diabetes is a kind of punishment, one that will cause you to live a shorter life?

Adolescent: Yeah.

Adult: I had no idea you felt this way. Would now be a good time for a talk about all this? [Discussion ensues.]

In this conversation, an adolescent clearly sees the downside of having a chronic illness. In addition to taking medications, he must watch what he eats, making him not always fun to be around (according to him). His parent empathizes but is not suffering as much with his disease as his son is with his. Yet, he meets his son where he (the son) is when he begins to catastrophize that he'll never get married or will die young. He can see that his son needs a longer discussion not only about his illness but also about God's role in it and is willing to invest the time in that discussion.

Chapter 4

Children's Questions about Loved Ones

Five to Eight Years Old

Can I talk to Daddy in heaven? (5 B)
Can I go to heaven with mommy? (6 G)
Why can't [NAME] come back to life? (6 G)
Why must my dad work late? (8 G)

Nine to Twelve Years Old

Why does my dad drink so much? (10 G)
Why do people in my family have babies when they're young? (11 G)
Will my dad lose his job? (11 G)
Why can't I live with my dad? (11 B)
Why can't my dad get a job? (11 B)

Adolescents

Why can't my mother forgive and let go of the past? (16 G)

INTRODUCTION

Children and teens are concerned about their loved ones. Even when they are not getting along with them, that concern is still present. Just like an adult who secretly inquires about someone with whom she's had an argument, children and teens realize that there is—or should be—a connection with those about whom they care. They want those whom they love to be well and happy. They want them to love them in return. Oftentimes, they want to be with their loved ones. Children and teens understand that it is not always easy to get along with their loved ones. Yet, they usually still want those loved ones in their lives. No wonder, then, that it is devastating for a child or teen to have no further communication with a loved one, such as when a parent has died.

Children and teens often fail to understand what their parents do that's seriously wrong (e.g., drink to excess, do drugs, fail to forgive others) and even the more mundane things, such as working late all the time. They don't understand the pressures on adults and the ways adults react to those pressures. Questions to God about such issues highlight the reality that young people think that only God has an answer for why things are the way they are.

WHAT THE SURVEYS REVEAL

In general, the questions posed by children and teens about loved ones are not happy ones. Nor are they merely ones borne out of curiosity. Rather, they are about death, illness, conflict, violence, and insecurities about being loved, in other words, the young people's own experiences. In many cases, these themes appeared in many of the children's and teens' responses to other questions on the questionnaires.

QUESTIONS

Family Members

Five to Eight Years Old

> *Why can't my family be happy? (5 G)*
> *Why can't my daddy be nice to me? (8 G)*
> *Why does my sister [brother] hit me? (8 B)*

Nine to Twelve Years Old

Why is [RELATIVE] so mean to me? (9–12)
Do parents ever stop fighting? (9 B)
Why does my dad yell at me so much? (9 G)
Why do parents fight? (9 G)
Why do my parents hate me? (9 G)
Why is my dad always in a bad mood? (11 G)
Why are you letting my parents get divorced? (11 G)
Can my parents get back together? (11 G)

Adolescents

Why is my family falling apart more and more each day? (13 G)
Why can't my parents like each other? (14 G)
Why do my parents keep fighting? (17 G)

The desire for young children to have a "normal" family is enormous, and their questions for God reflect this. From a five-year-old's "Why can't my family be happy?" to an eight-year-old's "Do parents ever stop fighting?" young children have a great deal of difficulty with adults who cannot (or will not) get along and create a peaceful home. Even the youngest children *do* notice when parents work late, drink, become angry over little things, and worry about money. Although most parents wouldn't think that young children pay attention to money matters, the fact that more than one child raised the question that an eight-year-old girl did: "Will my family stay out of debt?" is eye-opening.

Permitting children to express their fears is important. An adult should not respond to such fears with a dismissive "Don't be silly" or "Don't worry about it." After all, the fears are real, not silly. Children might have heard about other families who have experienced divorce, hard economic times, or illness, and they are concerned that this could happen to their family as well. In answering such questions, listening for the children's real concerns is necessary, so that we can address what's really on their minds. The sad truth is that people aren't always happy and that sometimes people argue. This doesn't always mean, however, that they don't love each other. Yet, sadly, when parents fight, they might not love each other and might even hate each other. And, despite what adults think, children see the pain and hatred and are grieved by it. In responding to these questions, we can provide reassurance when appropriate and empathy in every case.

Conflict in the home is also an important matter to older children. Their questions reflect the pain that they experience. These questions, addressed to God, should give us all pause. What kind of lives do many children have? Is their home a safe haven, or is it a terrifying place? Do parents love them, or do they ignore them? "Why do my parents hate me?" wondered a nine-year-old girl. Whether or not her parents hate her, she feels that they do and has asked God this question. As we answer such questions, we need to demonstrate the humility that recognizes that we do not always have answers that satisfy the needs of children. Furthermore, we must be careful not to speak badly of the parents without all the facts. Children yearn to be loved by their parents, and they can idealize even the cruelest of parents. It is not our place to tear down the relationship between the child and parent. On the other hand, if we believe that the child is being abused or mistreated in some way, we must act to protect the child by contacting local protective services.

Conflict might be caused by economic reasons, and, as stated above, children are usually aware of economic problems facing the family: "Will dad lose his job?"; "Why can't dad get a new job?" In addition to the tension in the home that unemployment can foster, children are also aware that there is not enough money to purchase the things that used to be so plentiful, including new clothes and food. In answering such a question, we can provide hope rather than a dire prediction based on the latest unemployment statistics.

Like younger children, adolescents often pose questions related to family dissolution because of illness or conflict. One can almost hear the pain in the thirteen-year old's voice as she asked, "Why is my family falling apart more and more each day?" Whether due to parental fighting or disgust, or due to mental illness, the adolescent clearly knows how she wants life to be and how far short of that mark her family falls. Teens can't understand why parents can't just get along and forgive each other. Such a teen needs a person to listen to her dismay.

Loved Ones Who Are Not Present

Five to Eight Years Old

Will my dad be safe at war? (6 G)

Will my sister be safe when she drives? (6 B)
Is my mom going to die? (7 G)
Will my family stay healthy? (7 G)
Will [NAME] get better? (8 G)
Will my family stay out of debt? (8 G)
Will my brother ever grow up? (8 B)
Will my dad ever live with us again? (7 G)
Will I ever see [NAME] again? (5–9)

Nine to Twelve Years Old

Why did my father leave me? Will he ever come back? (9–12)
Why don't my parents ever visit me? (9 B)
What's my real mother like? (11 G)

When living loved ones are absent from their lives, children wonder where they are and if they're OK. Children long for the security of those who gave them life, those who should be the closest people to them. Yet, some children feel neglected and forgotten: "Why don't my real parents ever visit me?" Imagine the pain of the child who believes that his own parents care so little for him that they have forgotten him. When we answer such questions, we must do our best to preserve the love that the child has for the parent, even as we discuss errant parents. Again, having the facts about a situation makes it more likely to provide a more truthful answer. Under no circumstances should we let our own biases and prejudices color the response we give. After all, our biases and prejudices are our problem, not a child's.

Concern about the health of family members is not just about parents but about siblings as well. As a rule, young children don't like it when family members are separated—whether by conflict, illness, or death. "Will dad ever live with us again?" wondered a seven-year-old. For the children who posed a question as did a six-year-old ("Will my dad be safe at war?"), there is fear that the separation might be permanent. For the most part, children believe that wars are stupid, and when a parent is sent to war, they feel loss and terror, especially if they have seen pictures or images on television or the internet from war-torn lands. Even temporary separations necessitated by the need for parents to work late (and spend less time at home) are worrisome to young children; they are afraid a parent will never come home again. We can explain the reason that a parent works late and reassure the child that he or she will be home as soon as possible.

Loved Ones Who Are Ill

Why does my [RELATIVE] have [DISEASE]? (9–12)
Can [Name] be healed of cancer? (10 G)
Why did my best friend's mom get COVID? (10 B)
Why do you let my mom be so sick? (10 G)
Will my brother ever be able to walk? (11 B)
Why did you let my brother be born blind? It's not fair! (11 G)
Is Mom going to get cancer again? (12 G)

Like the questions about illness that children and teens asked about themselves (as discussed in the prior chapter), illness deeply troubles young people. Cancer is such a terrible disease; why must the people whom children love have it? Why can't they be cured of it? And if they are cured, will it ever return again? The children are asking profound existential questions; they are not asking about scientific theories of cancer or any other disease. Furthermore, when they see their sisters and brothers affected by a condition which they themselves do not have, they wonder why. What is the purpose of their sibling being so ill or affected? Will their sibling have a future? In answering these questions, we might ask children for their ideas about why people are ill in order to discern whether they have erroneous ideas, such as illness is a punishment. Then, we can answer their questions as honestly as we can.

Deceased Loved Ones

Is [NAME] OK in heaven? (5–8)
Why did you let [NAME] die? (9–12)
Why does my family have so many funerals? (9 G)
Can I speak to [a dead relative]? (9 G)
What was [dead relative] like? (9–10)
Does my uncle still have only one leg in heaven? (9 G)
Can I see my dead brother? (10 B)
Will you bring my mom back to life? (10 G)
Is Mom happy in heaven? (10 B)

Do people have cancer in heaven? (10 G)
Will you tell me about my father who died? (11 G)
Who killed my mom? (12 B)
Can my aunt and uncle ever have a healthy baby? (12 G)
How is my brother and sister who never got to live? (12 G)
  [miscarriage]

Adolescents

When will my mom die? (14 G)
Why do the people I love all die? (14 G)
Why do people die by others' mistakes? (14 G)

Many questions centered on death, reflecting the children's desire for the absent person and their concern that the person is in heaven and is now OK. Children want to know where their deceased relatives are and whether they can see or speak to them. They wonder whether the dead are free of the physical problems that they had while on earth and whether they are happy. We can assure them that a deceased loved one does not suffer as they did while alive. Children often ask God to bring a deceased person back to life, a request that obviously cannot be granted. If a child did not know the deceased relative personally, he might ask God what the person was like. A chilling question posed by a twelve-year-old boy ("Who killed my mom?") makes one realize that not only do some children suffer because of the loss of a parent but they also suffer because of the violence and suddenness of the death. In answering such a question, we would want to listen well to the child's pain and to provide answers that would give comfort and perhaps refer him to a professional who can assist in his care. Some children have had more than their share of death, as epitomized by one child's question: "Why does my family have so many funerals?"

Adolescent death-related questions are especially poignant and reflect sadness, frustration, and anger. The adolescent is beginning to realize how very little control she (or any adult for that matter) has over the fate of loved ones. We can certainly commiserate with her feelings. Death is difficult for most of us to contemplate.

In answering all such questions, we can reassure children and teens that their loved one is safe and is no longer in pain.

On the opposite end of life, a number of young people wondered why babies do not live: "Can my aunt and uncle ever have a healthy baby?" and "How are my brother and sister who never got to live?" Although many babies do not live because they have congenital problems, that is not true of all. In answering such questions, one might say that we don't know why all babies can't live but that we know they are not suffering where they are. A striking question is one posed by an eleven-year-old girl: "Why do people in my family have babies when they're young?" Does she fear that she will be next? An adult hearing such a question can reassure her that she does not have to have a baby when she is young, providing guidance on what she can do to ensure that this does not happen.

Unhealthy Habits

Can you make [NAME] stop smoking? (9 G)
Why does my mom [dad] drink, and why don't you stop her? (7 B)
Why is my dad so mean when he drinks? (10 G)
Why is my mother a witch when she drinks? Why can't she stop drinking? (13 G)

Addictions, especially the use of alcohol, are noted by the children, who wonder why the parent must drink and why God doesn't stop him or her. This is especially true if the parent under the influence treats the child badly. In general, children think the use of alcohol and drugs is stupid, but they are too inexperienced to understand why the parent can't simply stop drinking or using. In answering this type of question, we can help young people think of addictions as a type of illness, all the while empathizing with their pain. If there is the suspicion that a child is being abused in any way, protective services must be involved.

Suggesting Abuse

Why does Mommy hit me hard? (5 B)
Can you make Daddy unmad when he gets mad at me? (5 G)
When am I too old to be hit? (10 B)

Unfortunately, a number of questions focused on violence (in action or in word) in the home. Although one might argue that siblings have always struck each other and corporal punishment was probably harsher in previous times than it is now, the home is no place for violence of any kind. We now know that trauma of any kind can have lasting effects on children and adults alike, but that children and teens are especially vulnerable to the effects of trauma because of their developing brains. And why shouldn't they be vulnerable? They are relatively helpless to stop the trauma being inflicted on themselves or loved ones. They learn to live life in fear; they learn to see the world as a scary place; they lose the ability to fully trust others.

If it seems that the child is being abused, protection of that child is in order. As in the advice given in the previous set of questions, if there is suspicion that a child is being abused in any way, protective services must be sought.

Being Loved, Cared for, Remembered

Will Mom and Dad ever love me? (6 B)
Does anyone in my family care about me? (7 B)
Why do my parents sometimes forget all about God? (7 G)

Perhaps the most devastating are questions like these. Rather than seeing these questions as just the usual wonderings of children, it is important to note that the vast majority of children did not raise these questions. Yet, the fact that they were raised by younger children is even more worrisome. Reassurance is in order as we answer the questions, unless reassurance would obviously be false. In such cases, an appropriate answer would be "I don't know, but I hope so. I care about you." Children who are in home situations in which they experience little love or care need professional assistance. In responding to the question about why parents forget God, we might say that although it is not good to forget God, sometimes adults have so much on their minds that they seem to have forgotten God. In those situations in which parents have actually abandoned God, we can commiserate with the child and remind him that God will never forget the parents (or the child), no matter what they do.

SAMPLE CONVERSATIONS

In the following examples, the goal is to permit the child to give voice to his or concerns and questions about family members. Obviously, responses must be matched to a child's age, temperament, and level of cognitive development. In some cases, reassurance is all that is needed; in other cases, a discussion is in order. Each hypothetical conversation is followed by the important points that it is meant to demonstrate.

Five to Eight Years Old

Child: Will my mom and dad ever love me?

Adult: Why do you think that they don't love you?

Child: They get mad at me a lot.

Adult: I'm sorry that's happening. That must be hard for you. Why do they get mad?

Child: When I don't feed the dog. I think they like the dog better than they like me.

Adult: I don't think so. But they're probably afraid that the dog won't be fed. Then the dog could get sick.

Child: I don't want the dog to get sick, but I still don't think they love me.

Adult: Lots of times, parents raise their voices at their children because they want them to do the right things. But that doesn't mean that they don't love their children. It just means that they're annoyed or are having a bad day. Those parents are sorry after they raise their voices.

Child: My mom said she was sorry last week after she yelled at me.

Adult: When she did that, what did you say?

Child: I hugged her. And she smiled.

Adult: See what I mean?

Child: It felt good.

Adult: What are some ways that you can remember to feed the dog so that your parents won't be upset? [Discussion ensues.]

In this conversation, a young child feels like his parents like the family dog more than him because they get upset when he forgets to feed the dog; young children often forget to feed their pets. (In this conversation, the child has not reported abuse, which would be a reportable occurrence.) The adult reassures the child that his parents do love him but identifies what his parents' concern is. She points out that parents sometimes raise their voices to get their children's attention, not because they do not love them. In giving the child reasons for parental behavior and pointing out they are often sorry for what they said, the adult's words remind the child that his mother apologized to him for raising her voice at him. The adult then furthers the learning from this episode to strategize with this child ways that he can remember to feed the dog, ensuring a more peaceful existence for all. Including him in the strategy reminds the child that he is part of the solution, a valuable lesson at any age.

* * *

Child: I'm so sad.

Adult: You miss your mom?

Child: Uh-huh. I hope she's OK in heaven.

Adult: I'm sure she is.

Child: Do you think that I'll see her again one day?

Adult: Yes, I do. I believe that all of us will see the people whom we love the most after we die.

Child: Will she look different? Will I know who she is?

Adult: I think you will.

Child: Will she know who I am, even if I grow up . . . and have a beard?

Adult: She will always know who you are, because a mother can never forget her child.

Child: I feel better, but I wish she was still alive.

Adult: I know you do, and I wish that, too.

When parents die, it is a crushing blow for children of all ages. Many children are concerned that their parents won't know them as they grow up. In this conversation, that is exactly the concern of the child. He misses his mother but is afraid that she will no longer know him as he grows up. The adult is completely and constantly empathetic with the child, gently reassuring him as she lets the child know that death does not break the mother-child bond.

* * *

Child: I don't like that Daddy has to go away.

Adult: I don't like it either. Do you know why he has to go away?

Child: He's in the Army, and they told him he had to go. I'm scared.

Adult: Of what?

Child: That he'll get hurt. Or never come back.

Adult: We need to pray for him every day.

Child: I will, but do you think he'll forget me?

Adult: How could he forget you?

Child: Maybe he just will.

Adult: He loves you so much. He will never forget you. Never. Would you like to say a prayer for him right now? And then maybe you can write him a little note about how much you love him.

Child: Will you help me do it?

Adult: Of course.

Unfortunately, in our world, many parents are called to active military service. In this conversation, a young child has both understandable fears for her father's safety and unrealistic fears he will forget her. The adult reassures her and offers to pray with her for her father's safety. Then, the adult suggests a concrete action that the child can do to show her father that she loves him.

Nine to Twelve Years Old

Child: Why did God let my brother be born blind? He didn't do anything wrong.

Adult: Do you think that people are blind because they did something wrong?

Child: Isn't that what the Bible says?

Adult: No. In fact, Jesus told his friends that just because someone was ill or had a problem didn't mean that he or she did anything wrong.

Child: But why did God let my brother be blind?

Adult: I don't know, but I believe that God isn't happy that your brother is blind.

Child: But can't God fix it so he can see? God can do anything, and Jesus made people see.

Adult: I know, but that doesn't seem to be the way God works now.

Child: I don't think it's fair. My little brother is cute. Cute children shouldn't have problems.

Adult: You're a good sister to him. In a way, God's love for your brother comes through you.

Child: But I can't make him see!

Adult: You can't make his eyes better, but you can make him feel better, just by being you.

Child: Yeah . . . I guess you're right. But I still don't like it.

Adult: I don't blame you; I don't like it either.

Children often wonder why one member of the family has an illness or condition and others do not. In this conversation, an elementary school-age child is disturbed that her little brother is blind because he did something wrong; the adult rightly reassures her that this is not the case. In response, the child wants to know why God doesn't make him see; he's "cute," she says. Wisely, the adult does not pretend to have easy answers but, instead, praises her sisterly devotion, while commiserating that he (the adult) doesn't like the situation either, thus forging a bond between adult and child and helping the sister to better understand what she can do for her brother.

* * *

Child: I've been thinking about my brother and sister who died.

Adult: What have you been thinking about?

Child: They died while they were inside my mom. They were almost ready to be born, but they died. Do you think they know who I am?

Adult: Even though they didn't when they were inside your mom, I bet they do now.

Child: Really?

Adult: I believe that when people die they know a lot more than they did when they were on the earth.

Child: But my brother and sister weren't even born yet!

Adult: But they are still God's children. It doesn't matter how old they were when they died.

Child: I like that. I like that they know who I am. Maybe I'll see them one day in heaven.

Adult: I'm sure you will.

Child: That would be cool.

At elementary school age, children not only realize death is irreversible, but they also start to understand the loss of life before babies are born. In this conversation, an older sibling mourns the loss of his twin siblings and worries that they will never know him (and he will not know them). This is VERY important for children this age! The adult reassures the child that he will meet them in heaven and that they will indeed know each other, which obviously pleases the child, teaching him a lesson that family bonds are not broken by death.

Adolescents

Adolescent: Why do all the people that I love die?

Adult: I'm so sorry. I know that you're going through a rough time.

Adolescent: Why would God do this to me?

Adult: Do you really think that God is doing this to you?

Adolescent: Well, I'm the one who is sad all the time. I'm the one who lost my dad, and then, my grandmother, and then my best friend and her mother. I feel beat up.

Adult: I would feel like that, too. But God doesn't make people die to punish someone.

Adolescent: It sure feels like that to me. Sometimes I get mad at God and don't want to pray to him anymore. Do you think that God hates me for doing that?

Adult: No, we know that God is love. God doesn't hate anyone. And even some of the prophets and the psalms describe not wanting or being able to pray. Sometimes I don't feel like praying.

Adolescent: Really?

Adult: Absolutely. I believe that God understands why we feel like that sometimes.

Adolescent: I still wish so many people hadn't died.

Adult: I know. I know. [Further discussion ensues.]

This conversation focuses on two issues. The first is that the teen is grieving, experiencing many deaths in her life, and wondering if God is directly doing this to her. When the adult emphasizes with the teen, she then confesses that she doesn't feel like praying and wonders if God hates her for that. Rather than giving a sermon, the adult simply says that he doesn't always feel like praying and that God understands because God is love. The adult commiserates with the teen's distress and invites further conversation. Further conversation is imperative here, as a young person with so many losses may need professional grief counseling.

* * *

Adolescent: Why is my family falling apart more and more?

Adult: What do you mean?

Adolescent: First, my brother was doing drugs, and now my mom and dad are separating.

Adult: I'm really sorry.

Adolescent: I hate my life. Why is God letting this happen?

Adult: It's hard knowing that your family is having a lot of problems and God can do everything but doesn't seem to help your family.

Adolescent: Yeah, why doesn't God solve the problems? Like, why doesn't God make my brother sick when he does drugs so he wouldn't do them anymore? Since God is love, why doesn't God make my mom and dad love each other again?

Adult: Because God doesn't interfere with human free will.

Adolescent: I don't think human free will is worth it, do you? So many people do so many bad things, things that hurt other people. God should just stop them.

Adult: How would God pick which people to stop?

Adolescent: The ones who were going to hurt themselves or other people.

Adult: That wouldn't be free will, would it? Free will means that people can freely choose what to do, right or wrong, good or bad. You like your free will, right?

Adolescent: Yeah, but I'm not hurting other people. It's so complicated being grown up.

Adult: It certainly is. [Discussion ensues.]

Adolescents hate when their families are "falling apart." In this conversation, a teen makes that statement, for which the adult rightly requests clarification. When she hears about the issues in the teen's life, she expresses sorrow and restates the teen's disappointment with God's inaction. The teen (naturally) feels that God should step in, and when God does not, the teen is understandably upset. The talk about free will is an important one that needs to occur, as it is mentioned so frequently by older children and adolescents. The adult's acknowledgement that it IS hard to be an adult further strengthens the bond between teen and adult, who will be more likely to turn to this adult in the future because of the empathy shown here.

* * *

Adolescent: I've come to the conclusion that my parents never loved me.

Adult: What made you come to that conclusion?

Adolescent: They never ask about my day at school. They never ask about my friends. Sometimes, I feel invisible.

Adult: Do your parents know you feel this way?

Adolescent: Nope.

Adult: Do they yell at you?

Adolescent: They ignore me; that's it. Just like God ignores me.

Adult: How does God ignore you?

Adolescent: Never answers my prayers. Never gives me a good feeling about myself. Like, I know a girl who says when she prays, she feels "lighter." I feel nothing. So, I've given up on God, just like I've given up on my parents. It's me against the world, that's for sure.

Adult: I'd like to talk a lot more about this with you, if you have the time and want to.

Adolescent: Sure . . . what do I have to lose?

Unfortunately, many parents are not overtly abusive to their children, but they may ignore them out of being immersed in their own issues or because they are simply ignorant of the needs of their children. If parents ignore a teen, it is natural for him to believe that God may be uninterested in him as well. The adult in this conversation realizes that much more needs to be discussed and asks the teen whether he would like to further the conversation. This may be the first real interest that anyone has taken with this teen. And although his response sounds lackadaisical, it is more likely that he is afraid of being hurt by another person, so he doesn't want to come off as too eager or needy. In other words, if one promises to talk with a child or teen, keep the promise. Be sure to understand what a child or teen is trying to communicate; if he or she is being harmed or might harm self or another, mental health referral is imperative.

Chapter 5

Children's Questions about Evil

Why don't you kill off bad people? (8 B)
Why don't you make people do what you want them to do? (10 B)
Why do you let the devil keep hurting us? (10 G)
Why don't you stop wars? (12 G)
Why do bad things happen? I want to know from you and not from a textbook. (16 G)
I wouldn't ask a question as I might be scared to know the answer. (16 G)

INTRODUCTION

Evil frightens us, and if it doesn't, it should. As adults, we may be very concerned about crime and violence in our neighborhoods, and the situation in our world where insurrections, coups, and wars seem to be never-ending. Why must this be? Why must human beings do evil to others and to the places in which they live? As adults, we understand the misuse of human free will and greed that lead to evil acts. We may wonder, "How did all this evil get into the world? From where does it come?" In fact, when we hear about a particularly diabolical act of evil, we are aghast; how did someone even conceive of such an act, let alone carry it out?

Children and adolescents have many fears about evil. They look to us for answers and often find few. For young people who have been raised in a Christian tradition, they have heard of the devil and that the devil is the source of all evil. They may be afraid of the devil or, alternatively, demonstrate much bravado when describing what they would do to it. But why does an all-powerful God let the devil have so much power? How did the sin of Adam and Eve (i.e., eating a forbidden fruit) lead to all this? Similarly, these children have learned about hell, and it scares them. Who ends up there . . . and why?

The role of God in all this puzzles children. If God is all good and all powerful, why doesn't God simply eradicate evil? It surely would make life easier for all, and it has been a question that theologians have asked throughout the ages. Is God really for us? Can God be trusted?

WHAT THE SURVEYS REVEAL

The questions in this section are about evil in general, even if it is not directly experienced by the child or teen. Evil in the world troubles children and teens greatly. Why must it exist? If God is good and created everything, how does evil have such a hold on our world? Although younger children have many questions about the devil (Who is he? Why is he like this?), older children and teens wonder more about the consequences of Adam and Eve's sin, the existence of hell, and the reality of personal sin.

QUESTIONS

The Devil and Hell

How did the devil become the devil? (7 B)
Is the devil real? (8 B)
Has the devil tried to sneak into heaven? (10 B)
Can the devil take over our bodies? (11 G)
Why do people hate God and worship Satan? (13 B)
What's hell like? (8 B)
Does hell burn eternally? (10 G)
Who is in hell? (10 B)
What does it take to get to hell? (11 G)
Is there really a hell? (multiple)

Explaining the devil to young children is a bit tricky—one wants to answer their questions without frightening them into believing that the devil is a little creature with a pitchfork. It is important for children to know that evil is in the world and that the Christian tradition speaks of an evil spirit which definitely does not look like the cartoon characters of devils that we have seen. We need to reassure young children that the devil doesn't take over the bodies and minds of children.

Explaining hell to young people must also be done with care. The traditional images of fire and smoke would be frightening to anyone, especially a small child. But it must be acknowledged that different Christian traditions have different interpretations of hell. In addition, although we want to communicate that hell is reserved for those who reject God, we don't want to give the impression that children's minor transgressions merit eternal damnation. On the other hand, even these minor transgressions might be sins in the sense of a young person turning away from God.

At the same time that we are discussing sin, it is also wise to highlight God's love and mercy. It is important for young children to know that God is just, but that God does not keep score. God is always ready to forgive. God does not want us to turn away from him, and God will never turn away from us.

Human Evil

Why is there so much crime? (8 G)
Will there ever be a time when there are no more wars? (9 B)
Will evil ever overcome good? (11 B)
Why is there sin and evil? (12 B)
Why is there hate? (12 B)
Why is there so much evil in the world? (12 B)
Why are people mean and nasty? (8 B)
Why do people kill each other? Why do people kill animals? (8 G)
[After 9/11] Why did those people hurt our people? (9 B)
Why were guns invented? (10 B)
Do evil people ever get to heaven? (11 G)
Why do people hurt each other intentionally and feel no remorse?
  (17 G)

The presence of evil in our world is obvious but is still a mystery. From where does evil come? How does the pervasive evil in our world square with a loving and good God? Just as we adults have difficulty with these questions, so too do children and teens, and maybe even more so. They truly don't understand why the world must be the way it is. The attraction of so many human beings to evil is, indeed, baffling. Older children and teens wonder how evil entered the world, and they fear that evil will ultimately win over good, which is a frightening prospect. Many people have no difficulty in hurting others in any way that they can imagine, and they have a variety of reasons for inflicting the evil. Yet, evil is still evil, regardless of its underlying reason. When discussing questions that deal with why certain people did certain acts, we do well to encourage children and teens to share their perspectives with us. Young people need to learn that although we can have explanations for evil, we can never have excuses for it. Evil in our world is a reality with which young people must come to terms so that they will not be swept up in its wake. A good way to accomplish this is to encourage young people to discuss the evil that they see and hear about.

God's Role in the Existence of Evil

Why don't you kill off the bad people? (8 B)
Why do you let people be bad? (12 G)
Why don't you stop the violence and the terrorists? (12 B)

Thirteen Years and Older

Why do bad things happen? I want to know from you and not from a textbook. (16 G)
I wouldn't ask a question as I might be scared to know the answer. (16 G)

The events of September 11, 2001, made a lasting impression on many young people, especially those who were of elementary school age at the time of the attack. "Why did our people get hurt?" many children wondered. For the first time, many children witnessed human-devised evil on a large-scale basis. The hatred that they witnessed troubled them greatly. They wonder why God didn't (and doesn't) protect the innocent. They wonder why God lets people hate other people and do bad things. Most of all, they wonder why an all-good God doesn't stop all the violence, hate, and evil. Although they have a better understanding of human free will than when they were younger, they still can't understand why God doesn't override that free will to protect the innocent. This is an issue that the human authors of Scripture grappled with as well.

Sin

Are there really sins? (8 B)
What was the first sin—really? (10 B)
Is cussing really a sin? Why? (12 B)

The word "sin" is a common one used by Christians to describe acts that are wrong. Young people want to know about sins—what actions are sins, what the first sin was, and how many sins it takes to deserve hell. Their questions should be answered as honestly as possible, with the use of "I don't know" when appropriate. They can be reminded that no one has seen hell and that all sins are not equal in magnitude.

For example, a child asks if lying is a sin. The answer is yes, because lying takes us away from God who is Truth. The child then asks if all lies take us away from God the same distance. The answer is no. The lie of the child who lies about breaking a vase or not doing his homework is not equal to the lie of someone who falsely denies that he murdered someone and who pins the blame on someone else. Although both examples illustrate an individual trying to deny something that he had done, the deeds (breaking a vase vs. murdering someone) are not equal in seriousness. In addition, the murderer is trying to hurt another person by pinning the blame on him. Sins that blame another individual have the capacity to hurt that person and so involve greater culpability than sins that do not involve others.

Adam and Eve's Influence on Sin

Why is Adam and Eve's sin such a big deal? (11 G)
What if Adam and Eve hadn't eaten the apple? (11 B)
Why are we stuck with Adam and Eve's mistake? (11 B)
What if Adam and Eve never sinned? (12 G)

Why do people have to suffer because of Adam and Eve? (13 G)
Why didn't Adam and Eve get a second chance? (15 G)
Why were you so hard on Adam and Eve? (17 G)

A specific area of interest to older children and teens is why Adam and Eve's sin continues to cause us so much trouble. Although younger children tend to focus on Adam and Eve ("Why are we stuck with Adam and Eve's mistake?"), adolescents focus on what seems to them God's severity in dealing with Adam and Eve ("Why didn't Adam and Eve get a second chance?"). This is probably an area that many adults have wondered about as well. Why did the transgression of ancient people have such an enduring effect on the human race? Why are we so attracted to evil? Asking for the impressions of young people might not only help us to better answer their questions but to also clarify our own beliefs.

SAMPLE CONVERSATIONS

In the following examples, the goal is to permit the child to give voice to his or concerns and questions about evil and sin. Obviously, responses must be matched to a child's age, temperament, and level of cognitive development. In some cases, reassurance is all that is needed; in other cases, a discussion is in order. Each hypothetical conversation is followed by the important points that it is meant to demonstrate.

Five to Eight Years Old

Child: Is there really a devil?

Adult: We believe that there is an evil spirit, but it doesn't look like the drawings that we see of devils. No one has seen that spirit.

Child: What's "evil" mean?

Adult: Very, very bad.

Child: How did it become so bad?

Adult: I'm not exactly sure. Some people think that the spirit was once an angel who didn't want to love and obey God anymore.

Child: Why didn't God destroy it?

Adult: I don't know.

Child: Where does the bad spirit stay?

Adult: In hell.

Child: Uh-oh. That's a bad word.

Adult: Well, sometimes grown-ups say it in a bad way, but it's where the bad spirit is.

Child: Who else is there? Where is it?

Adult: We don't know.

Child: What's it like?

Adult: We don't know because no one has ever seen it. Some people think that it might be full of fire and smoke, but that's not what the church teaches.

Child: I wouldn't want to be there!

Adult: Neither would I. And as long as we love and obey God, we won't be there.

It is not uncommon for young children to be afraid of evil or that which is bad. In this conversation, a young child asks questions about the devil. Because at her age, she can believe in almost everything, the devil is a very real entity. The adult answers her questions, comfortable enough to say "I don't know" when that is the case. In terms of hell, it IS a scary place for a young child, often because of pictures or videos they may have seen about it. Although a hot, fiery place might not be how we imagine hell, it is best not to speak in more abstract terms to a child of this age (e.g., hell is the eternal absence of God's presence) because of the degree of literality children of this age possess.

* * *

Child: What's a sin?

Adult: A sin is when you do something that moves you away from God. It can take you a little away or a lot away.

Child: What's a little away?

Adult: Taking something that belongs to your brother.

Child: What's a lot away?

Adult: Intentionally hurting someone just to hurt them.

Child: Do you do sins?

Adult: Sometimes I do. How about you?

Child: Maybe. Is making fun of someone who makes a mistake in school a sin?

Adult: Yes. Would God make fun of someone who made a mistake?

Child: No.

Adult: Then we shouldn't do it either because it's wrong and it hurts another person. But the very good news is that God always forgives us when we sin. We should ask God's forgiveness and also the forgiveness of anyone we think we hurt.

Child: Suppose the other person doesn't forgive? Does that change God's mind?

Adult: No. God still forgives.

In this conversation, a young child wants to know the meaning of the word sin. In simple terms, the adult helps the child understand that not all sins are the same and answers honestly when the child asks if he ever sins. This builds a bond between adult and child. When the child is asked if he ever sins, he responds by asking if a certain action is a sin; when told it is, the adult helps the child understand why it is a sin and assures the child of God's forgiveness. This is a very important lesson for young children.

Nine to Twelve Years Old

Child: What's the deal about all the bad people and bad stuff in the world?

Adult: What do you mean, "What's the deal"?

Child: Why are there so many bad people in the world? Why do they do such terrible things? And why doesn't God stop it all?

Adult: Well, people don't start out bad. Babies are good, right?

Child: Yeah . . .

Adult: And some people would say that there are no bad people, just people who do bad things.

Child: I think they are bad people, like people who kill other people.

Adult: It seems that way.

Child: But, OK, even if people aren't bad, they do bad things. Why do people want to do bad things, especially to other people?

Adult: It's very hard to understand, isn't it?

Child: Yeah.

Adult: We don't always understand why people do the things they do. Sometimes we don't even understand the things we do. Has that ever happened to you?

Child: Yeah. But I've never done anything really nasty.

Adult: I know you haven't.

Child: I just wish all the bad people would die. Why doesn't God get rid of them so the rest of us could live in peace?

Adult: Well, people who do bad things are God's children, too, just like we are.

Child: They sure don't act like it.

Adult: Well, that's true of everybody sometimes, but God continues to love us all and forgive us. God wants all of us to be with him forever.

Child: Yeah, but maybe some people don't want to be with God.

Adult: You're probably right. It's very sad.

Child: But why does God let people hurt other people? If he loves us, why does he let us get hurt by bad people?

Adult: I don't think God likes it when any of his children hurt each other, just like I don't like it when your brother and you fight.

Child: But you make us stop!

Adult: That's true. And I don't know why God doesn't stop it all sometimes. I know that I sure wish he would.

Child: Yeah, me too.

Why people do bad things is a mystery to elementary school–age children: why be so mean? In this conversation, the adult spends much time commiserating with the child's views, even while correcting misunderstandings. The adult doesn't give easy answers and remains with the child as he (the child) struggles with his questions about people doing bad things. Although children of this age can understand bad actions, they don't understand why people want to do them. When the child wishes that all the people who do bad things would die, the adult reminds the child that they are God's children (just like the child is), loved by God. Clearly, the child wants God to stop people from doing bad things and draws a comparison between what the parent does when he and his brother fight and what he thinks God should do. The adult completely empathizes with the child, creating greater bonding between the two.

* * *

Child: Why is cussing wrong?

Adult: It's disrespectful.

Child: Not always.

Adult: When you curse at a person, it is.

Child: Maybe they deserve it.

Adult: Are you saying that people deserve disrespect?

Child: Sometimes. Like if they call you a name, you call them one back with the cuss word in it.

Adult: Is that what God would do?

Child: People don't cuss at God, and if they did, he could just kill them.

Adult: People do curse at God and use God's name in bad ways. And God doesn't kill them off.

Child: God should!

Adult: No. God is love. Although God doesn't like the language, God shows mercy.

Child: If I were God and they used my name in a bad way, I'd get back at them.

Adult: How would you get back at them? [Discussion ensues.]

This conversation is an example of an elementary school-age child trying to figure out why something is wrong, in this case cursing. The child seems to think it's OK to curse at others if they brought it on themselves, a view that, unfortunately, many adults hold as well. The adult in this situation asks if this is what God would do. In response, the child shows her innocence in stating that people don't curse at God. When told that is not the case, the child opines that God should kill such people, to which the adult reminds her that God is love, and love does not behave that way. In asking the child how she would get back at people who wronged her, the adult has a window into a child's moral sense—what is acceptable retaliation and what is not. This is important information for the child to articulate aloud and for the adult to know.

Adolescents

Adolescent: You know what I don't get?

Adult: What?

Adolescent: The whole Adam and Eve thing. I mean, it was just an apple that they ate. They didn't kill each other. So, what's the big deal?

Adult: About?

Adolescent: Why do we have to suffer because of them? Why didn't God give them—and us—a break?

Adult: Well, sometimes we suffer because of something that we've done.

Adolescent: I get that, but I still think that God was hard on them. It was only an apple.

Adult: It was disobedience.

Adolescent: OK, they disobeyed God. But I heard that because of what they did, evil entered the world. How could that be right? That doesn't make sense.

Adult: You know how sometimes people use drugs one time and then they get hooked?

Adolescent: Yeah . . .

Adult: Once people do things that are wrong, sometimes they want to keep doing wrong things. It's like they can't resist or stop anymore. Some people think that the reason that there is so much evil in the world is that people got used to doing bad things and then they just kept doing them.

Adolescent: Are you saying that evil is contagious?

Adult: Some people would definitely think of it that way.

Adolescent: That's interesting. (Pauses) I'll have to think about that one for a while.

The story of Adam and Eve troubles many adolescents. Why would God punish everyone for what two individuals did; it just doesn't seem fair. In this conversation, the adult tries to move the adolescent away from thinking about one discrete act (eating the apple) and toward thinking about doing wrong as almost an addiction (there is a fancy name for this—concupiscence), an addiction that has a contagious quality to it. This leads the adolescent to consider this point of view and the overall presence of evil more deeply. Adolescence is precisely the time for young people to seriously consider their ideas about why the world is like it is . . . and maybe revise those views.

* * *

Adolescent: Is there really a hell?

Adult: Why do you ask?

Adolescent: I was thinking that if God is love, love wouldn't punish someone forever.

Adult: That's a good take on it. But here's my question: What if hell is our choice?

Adolescent: That's stupid.

Adult: No hear me out. What if hell is our decision to reject God forever?

Adolescent: Why wouldn't God override us?

Adult: Free will; God goes along with what we want.

Adolescent: But God knows that hell is not good for us.

Adult: Absolutely, but God also honors free will; that's why God gave it to us.

Adolescent: I need to think about this one, because the way I think, God's love should win out. [Discussion ensues.]

In this conversation, an adolescent raises the very valid point that if God is love, why would anyone be in hell? The adult counters with the notion that maybe human beings choose hell, which the adolescent finds ludicrous. Why would people be that stupid, and why wouldn't God intervene in that stupidity? As in earlier conversation examples, the notion of free will arises, and this is a lesson that not only adolescents and children need to grapple with but also adults. When is it acceptable to interfere in someone's free will? When is it unacceptable? All of us need to better understand that, not only for ourselves but also for society at large. Like many conversations with adolescents, this one ends with the adolescent needing to think about her idea more closely.

Chapter 6

Children's Questions about Suffering, Illness, and Death

Why did you invent colds? (7 G)
Why do you let COVID hang around and keep changing so we can't get rid of it? (9 G)
Do we get a new body in heaven? (10 G)
What do we do during everlasting life? (11 G)
Will everyone get to heaven when they die? (11 B)
Why do you take little kids so soon? (13–17)

INTRODUCTION

Few people choose to suffer and be ill. Yet suffering and illness are all around us. Many (if not most) of us live in fear and dread that illness will befall us and our loved ones. Although we can understand biologically why living creatures age and get sick, that understanding does not usually help us when it's our turn. We have all experienced helplessness as we watch our own health be compromised or as we watch the suffering of loved ones when they are ill or infirm. And, although—intellectually—we can understand that some illnesses are brought on by lifestyle choices, it still doesn't make it easier when those illnesses occur in our lives. In fact, it might make it worse as feelings of guilt accumulate. And when death occurs in a loved one, many of us are left with an empty hole in our hearts. Again, even though we clearly understand the inevitability of death, that understanding doesn't soften the blow when it's our loved ones who have died.

Young children are mystified by illness. How could a germ too tiny to be seen cause so much suffering? How could one's own body turn against itself or fail to protect itself from inner and outer threats? Why does God allow germs to exist? Why does God permit normal cells to become cancerous? Death is even more problematic. Young children believe in the reversibility of death until they are older or have witnessed death. But once they understand that death is a given, the questions arise. Why must this be? Does dying hurt? What happens once someone dies? Where are they? Many adults have had these same questions.

As for adolescents, most hate being sick because it takes them away from the people and activities they love. They feel cheated out of life by illness; they resent death, especially when it happens to someone they love or to someone their age. How can an all-powerful God let this happen? Parents are not supposed to die; young people are not supposed to die. It's just wrong. Many a young person has fallen away from faith because they prayed for a miracle for their loved one and didn't get it. The wise adult who hears questions about illness and death does more listening than speaking. It's not an easy topic for any of us.

WHAT THE SURVEYS REVEAL

The questions in this section are about illness and death in general, not in relation to loved ones. Very few young children have probing questions in this category, probably because adults try to shield them from the uglier side of life. As a rule, when young children do have such questions (e.g., Is there a cure for cancer? Why must people die?), it is because someone close to them is suffering in some way. So, they want to know why *their* someone has cancer, is dying, or has died. A gentle answer is that people get sick, and we don't always know why certain people get certain illnesses or why certain people die from their illnesses.

QUESTIONS

The Pervasiveness of Suffering

Why is life hard? (9 G)
Why can't life be fair? (12 G)
Why is life violent and unfair? (12 G)
Why is the world so messed up? (12 G)
Why is there so much tragedy? (12 B)
Why is childbirth painful? (12 G)
Why do some people suffer a lot more than others? (13 G)
Why do bad things happen to really good people? (14 G)
Why must people suffer physically and mentally? (16 G)
Why all the suffering? (16 G)

The questions children and teens raise are often the same questions that adults raise. Why is life hard? Why must we die? Why must we suffer when we are on this earth? Why must there be illness and pain? Because older children are simply more aware of the world around them than they were at a younger age, they are more likely to pose these questions, even if they have no one close to them who is suffering or ill. Like the young Buddha who was protected from the uglier side of life in his father's castle and was dismayed when he saw illness and death outside the castle walls, many children have been protected from the bad side of life and are greatly troubled when they meet it personally. We adults can commiserate with their feelings, as we share our own struggles with these issues.

The Reality of Sickness

Is there a cure for cancer? (multiple)
Why don't you make all sick people better? (multiple)
Why must people get sick? (7 G)
Why can't you tell us the cures to all the diseases? (9 G)
Why can't people be healthy until they die? (10 B)
Do you make people sick? (11 G)
Will there be a cure for cancer? (12 G)
Why are some people always sick? (12 G)
Why did you make diseases? (13 G)

Children and teens look around and see people suffering; sometimes, it's someone to whom they are related. Why must this be? This is especially wrenching for the child if he or she has prayed for the person suffering or knows that the person is good. The world is, indeed, "messed up," as one child noted. Why does God let this happen? This is a question with which many people—young and old—have struggled over thousands of years. There is no easy answer, but many opportunities for questions and discussion.

Death

Why must people die? (7–12)
If someone dies early, do they come back? (9 G)
Are people sad about being dead? (9 G)
Why do people die when they get shot? (9 G)
Is it scary to die? (10 G)
Why must innocent people die? (11 B)
Where do people go when they die? (11 B)
Where does a person's spirit go when he dies? (11 G)
What happens when we die? What's it like? (12 G)
Why are there so many deaths in the world? (12 G)
Why do good people die young and bad ones get to live? (12 B)
Why do some people die terribly? (12 G)

Young people have many questions about death and what happens after it. They cannot understand why any of us must die, especially from terrible diseases or violence at a young age. They wonder if dying is scary and if dead people are sad; they wonder where the dead are. They question why people must suffer so much before they die; why can't people stay healthy until the moment of their death? Sometimes our best response to these types of questions is "I don't know." Such conversations should not be rushed or brushed off. Asking children what they think frequently helps us to gather our own thoughts and to respond to them in an appropriate fashion.

God's Role in Illness and Death

Why did you make bodies that can be hurt? (10–11)

Why would you let bad things happen? (12 G)
Why do you permit pain and death? (13 B)

Although the Christian faith tradition teaches that the misery in the world is a result of the fallen nature of humanity, as was discussed earlier, children wonder why something that the first human beings did still affects people today. Other children wonder why an all-good, all-loving, all-powerful God doesn't step in and clean up the messiness of the world. That is another issue with which people have wrestled over thousands of years, another issue for which there is no easy answer.

One of the most difficult concepts for children of this age is why God permits bad things to happen. For example, although most children don't believe that God actually made someone drink and drive, they are mystified why God didn't stop it from happening. As one child said, "If God can do anything, why didn't God just make the drunk guy's car not start? Then, my dad would still be here."

God's Response to Intercessory Prayers for the Ill

I prayed for my dad. Why didn't you let him make it? (9 B)
Why don't you listen to my prayers? I don't want to hurt all the time (13 G)

A very frustrating aspect of human relationship with God in general and their own relationship with God in particular is why God doesn't answer prayers. As a nine-year-old boy complained, "I was praying for my teacher not to suffer so much. It wasn't like I was praying for something stupid. But she just got sicker and sicker. I got mad at God."

This is especially true since older children and teens are very aware of the concept of fairness, and for the most part, they believe that good people should be treated well, and people who fail to be good should be treated badly. In other words, people deserve what they get. So, when children see good people dying or suffering with various physical and emotional problems, they are confused and want to know why. If God made everything, then why did God make illnesses? If death is necessary, then why can't people just go to sleep and not wake up? In other words, why must so many deaths be preceded by suffering? So often, it seems to children (and perhaps to us as well) that good people die before "bad" people, the ultimate in unfairness. We can surely empathize with their dismay.

Answers loaded with platitudes don't work. Children are beginning to come to grips that the world is unfair and that suffering is part of human life. Hence, they need answers to their questions that permit them to ask more questions or, alternatively, speculate what might be going on. That takes time and patience; most of all, it takes ongoing conversations.

Children and teens do get some comfort from the knowledge that many, many people over thousands of years have wondered why life is unfair or full of suffering and death. They feel that they are in good company, even if adults don't know the answers. Yet, we cannot stop there. For example, merely telling young people that suffering is a "mystery" that many adults are unable to figure out doesn't really help them, because at a time when their cognitive abilities are maturing, they have a need to grapple with difficult topics. They need us to listen and, perhaps, even debate a few points with them.

If truth be told, we adults are frustrated by the pain and suffering in our world, and our own inability to fix it. We adults are stung when one of our loved ones is tormented by physical and emotional disorders, especially when we can do little to alleviate his or her suffering. We adults are distressed when good people die too soon, while those who seem to us "bad" go on as if nothing will ever happen to them. If it is hard for adults to accept what happens, how much more difficult is it for children who believe that adults can do much more than they can do, or who believe that God can do anything but chooses not to help?

Life can be beautiful, but life can also be wretched. How can we present both sides of life in such a way that young people don't end up depressed or anxious but still are aware of life's more difficult aspects? How can we be honest and at the same time compassionate in our explanations?

SAMPLE CONVERSATIONS

In the following examples, the goal is to permit the child to give voice to his or concerns and questions about suffering, illness, and death. Obviously, responses must be matched to a child's age, temperament, and level of cognitive development. In some cases, reassurance is all that is needed; in other cases, an ongoing discussion is in order. Each hypothetical conversation is followed by the important points that it is meant to demonstrate.

Five to Eight Years Old

Very few children of this age group had questions in this category, so only one will be offered as an example.

Child: Why doesn't God just make all sick people better?

Adult: What do you think?

Child: Maybe God doesn't want to! Maybe God wants to see people sick and sad.

Adult: Who told you that?

Child: No one. I just thought about it.

Adult: God made us to be healthy and happy.

Child: But lots of people aren't.

Adult: And sometimes we don't know why that is. Sometimes people are sick because they don't do something that would make them healthier, or they do something that makes them sick.

Child: I just think God should fix it all.

Adult: If you were God, what would you do? [Discussion ensues.]

In this conversation, a young child wants illness to go away and wants her powerful God to do something about it. Although the adult in this conversation points out that some illnesses are caused by human actions, that does not satisfy the child. In asking the child what she would do if she were God, the adult gives the child a chance to explain her thinking and the adult a chance to better understand and bond with her.

Nine to Twelve Years Old

Child: Why did God invent cancer?

Adult: God didn't invent cancer. Cancer happens when cells that aren't normal divide and make more of themselves. You learned about this in school, right?

Child: Yeah, but why aren't the cells normal?

Adult: Sometimes cells aren't normal because they're old or because they've been exposed to something that causes them to become abnormal.

Child: Why doesn't God stop it?

Adult: That's a good question, and I don't know why. Lots of people have asked the same question.

Child: If God knows everything, why doesn't God just tell us what the cure for cancer is?

Adult: I don't know, but there are lots of people working on it.

Child: Wouldn't it just be easier for God to tell us what the cure is?

Adult: Yes. But I think that God wants us to work with him in helping people get better. We're like his assistants.

Child: That's OK, but I wish that God would just tell us.

Adult: Me too.

Children cannot understand why an all-knowing God does not just give us answers to our problems; it seems cruel that God withholds such information. In this conversation, an elementary school-age child is perplexed that God just won't tell us what to do. In responding, the adult reminds the child that we work with God to make people better, which the child likes, but he is still haunted by God knowing and not telling us. The adult agrees, thus creating a greater bond with the child.

* * *

Child: Do you think that God is happy when people get sick?

Adult: No, I don't. God wants us to be healthy, not sick.

Child: Then, why doesn't God stop cancer and all kinds of sicknesses?

Adult: I'm not sure; what do you think?

Child: Maybe God doesn't want to. Or he can't.

Adult: Well, I think that God can stop illness, but I still don't know why he doesn't. It's really a hard thing to think about, isn't it?

Child: It sure is. I really don't like it.

This conversation is a bit different from the preceding one. The previous one is about God knowing the answer and not telling us; the current one is about whether God is pleased when people are ill, and (as the questions evolve) whether God wants to help people or even can do so. Again, the adult joins the child in the discomfort of the question, showing the child that even adults don't have all the answers.

* * *

Child: Why does God make us die?

Adult: God doesn't make us die. Death is the end of this life before the next one starts.

Child: Do you think it's scary to die?

Adult: Maybe for some people, but not for others.

Child: I hope that I don't die soon.

Adult: I don't think you will. You were OK at your last physical exam.

Child: Will you die soon?

Adult: I don't think so. Why do you ask?

Child: The father of a boy in my class died. He was in a car accident.

Adult: I'm very sorry to hear that.

Child: You'll be careful when you drive, OK?

Adult: I'll be very careful.

In this conversation, an elementary school–age child is clearly concerned about dying—how, when, who, why. His thoughts have been precipitated by the father of a classmate killed in a car accident. When the adult expresses regret for what happened to the father, the real purpose of the question surfaces: the child wants his own parent to be safe when driving because he doesn't want to suffer the same loss. The wrong thing to say here would be "Don't be silly," because if it happened to one parent, it could happen to his parent. Instead, the adult reassures the boy that she'll be careful when driving to ease his mind.

* * *

Child: Why is life unfair?

Adult: Life can be unfair but not always. Why are you thinking about this now?

Child: I saw a TV show about little kids in Haiti. They don't get enough to eat. There are gangs that kill people. It's a scary place, especially for kids.

Adult: That is unfair, isn't it?

Child: Yeah. Why doesn't God do something about them?

Adult: What should God do?

Child: Feed them! God knows how to make food. Then God could get rid of the gangs that hurt people.

Adult: Why do you think that God doesn't feed them or get rid of the gangs?

Child: I don't know, and it makes me sad that life is so hard for them.

Adult: Me too. I wish that God would make all the poverty, violence, and illness go away. Right now. But it doesn't happen. I don't know what we can do about the gangs, but in the meantime, there are charities that provide food for poor people all over the world. Maybe we could donate some money to them.

Child: Cool. Let's do that.

Adult: How about if I give something and you give something?

Child: Deal.

In this conversation, a child is troubled by the knowledge that children (perhaps of her own age or younger) go hungry and also could be hurt by gangs that want to do no good but only harm others. What a terrible way to live! Why doesn't God get involved? The adult agrees wholeheartedly with her, creating a bond, but the adult takes it much further than most children of this age could imagine because of their limited knowledge of the world and its resources. Acknowledging that there is little that those in one country can do about gangs in another country, the adult names something in which both child and adult CAN be involved—giving to charities that provide food for those in Haiti. This gives the child the agency to help others in some way, albeit a small one.

Adolescents

Adolescent: I'm really bummed out.

Adult: Why?

Adolescent: My best friend's father died of cancer. He was only 42!

Adult: That's very young. I'm sorry for you and your friend.

Adolescent: Thanks. But here's what I don't get. There are criminals who live a lot longer than my friend's dad. Mr. Ted was a good person. He even helped out at the homeless shelter until he got so sick. Criminals don't want to help people. So why does God let them go on as if everything is OK?

Adult: It's frustrating, isn't it? A man who did good things dies, and people who do bad things live. It doesn't make sense.

Adolescent: And another thing. Why doesn't God reward the good and punish the bad guys?

Adult: God does ultimately reward the good, and those who do evil will ultimately face judgment.

Adolescent: Ultimate is not good enough! I want it NOW!

Adult: You're frustrated over the death of your friend's dad.

Adolescent: Yes, I am. But I'm more frustrated over the fact that people who act in really evil ways do great. Like drug dealers—they have lots of money. They're doing great! And now, Mr. Ted's family might have to move because they don't have enough money to pay the bills.

Adult: It says in the Bible that God's ways are not ours, and our ways are not God's.

Adolescent: I know, and usually I'm OK with that. But not now. It sounds like a big excuse! I want God to act more like us.

Adult: What would that look like? [Discussion ensues.]

The topic of who dies when is very common in adolescence, especially when good people die young and people who do evil deeds seem to flourish. The adolescent in this conversation is obviously upset about the death of a friend's father and is incredulous that God would let criminals live. The adult does not lecture the teen but echoes her feelings. When the teen says she wants God to act more like human beings, the adult furthers the conversation by asking what that would look like.

* * *

Adolescent: Why does God let little kids and babies die?

Adult: What do you think?

Adolescent: I really have no idea. If I were God, I'd let them live.

Adult: Me too. But sometimes, babies and children have conditions and diseases that make life hard, and they die because of the conditions or illnesses.

Adolescent: But WHY are those conditions and diseases there in the first place? God could prevent them if God wanted to. It makes me nervous about God.

Adult: Nervous? How so?

Adolescent: Maybe God will want ME dead too soon! Maybe God will give me something that can't be cured and will kill me.

Adult: I'm sorry that this is bothering you so much.

Adolescent: I just wish I understood God a whole lot better. [Discussion ensues.]

This conversation is a bit different from the preceding one in that the issue is about the death of truly innocent people (babies, young children) and God's role in it. Adolescents no longer consider themselves children, and so they can look at children from afar, as it were. This teen in this conversation is nervous about a God who seems fickle; will this God suddenly decide that this teen should also die? Rather than dismissing the teen's thoughts as foolish, the adult empathizes and is open to greater conversation, which is certainly needed here and now, if the teen is open to it.

Chapter 7

Children's Questions about Creation and Nature

What do cats think about? (7 G)
What does the sun look like up close? (7 B)
How long was it before people showed up? (8 G)

What's at the end of the universe? (9 B)
How did the universe start? (10 G)
How old is the world? (12 B)
Will the ozone layer disappear? (12 B)
Did we evolve from apes? (12 G)
How many fish are there in all the oceans? (12 B)
Do dead things ever live again, come back to life? (12 G)

Why do you let us hurt the earth [planet]? (13 G)

INTRODUCTION

The grandeur of nature is amazing, but we adults are often too busy or too preoccupied to notice. We may see a new type of bird in our yard but are too busy to really take a good look. We may notice the gorgeous sunset but are too immersed in balancing our checkbook to go outside for a better view. We may hear about another species becoming extinct but are too preoccupied with keeping our own loved ones thriving to do very much about it.

Young children have a much different perspective. True, they don't have adult concerns and duties. But the truth is that they have something most of us lack: a sense of awe and wonder. Everything is new; everything is interesting. To them, it's never "just a bug"; it's a bug that they've never seen before. It's never "just some clouds"; it's clouds that look like something. It's never "just rain"; it's puddles to splash in. Children are interested in everything they see: everything is a miracle (although they wouldn't use that word). Children wonder how God thought up all the different varieties of . . . everything! They wonder how and when God first started creating and whether God still makes new things.

Adolescents wonder about God's motives. Why did God make insects and animals that can harm us? Why does God let poisonous plants exist? Why does God let bacteria and viruses that can hurt us flourish and spread? Is it a test? Is it punishment? It is mostly adolescents who pose such questions as "Are we alone?" and "Are we the only ones?" and who worry about when (and how) the earth will end. Younger children usually don't have the concept that all we see might—one day—no longer exist. Their ideas of aliens from other planets might come from cartoons.

Yet, older children and adolescents do not understand how people can pollute, destroy forests, or kill animals. We adults might understand the human motives behind these activities, but like young people, we might not understand natural disasters. Why must the earth's core fracture? Why must tornadoes exist; can't we stop them? Why must there be hurricanes and tsunamis?

If we listen carefully to children's and teens' questions about nature and all creation, we might regain a little bit of our own innocence from long ago.

WHAT THE SURVEYS REVEAL

Younger children wonder about why specific creatures are the way they are, while teens wonder about why there must be animals that hurt human beings and human beings who hurt the earth. In general, younger children want concrete answers, while older children and teens want more philosophical ones (even though very few teens had a question that related to nature).

QUESTIONS

Science

Why are clouds white? (5 G)
How do leaves stay on the trees? (5 G)
Why is grass green? (6 G)
What is fire made of? (6 B)
Where does the sun come from? (7 B)
What killed the dinosaurs? (8 B)

Some of the questions posed by children can be answered with reputable print or online sources (e.g., why are clouds white; why is grass green). We can take advantage of such sources of knowledge to educate ourselves as well.

The Origin of Various Creatures

How did you make seeds, flowers, trees, animals, dinosaurs, birds,
   people, snow, stars, moon, planets, etc.? (5–7)
Why did you make so many different types of dogs, [cats, flowers,
   trees, people]? (6–8)
How do things come alive? (5 B)
Did you divide something in two to make the earth? (8 B)
Are you still making new stuff? (8 G)
Did you really make it all in seven days? (11 B)

Much harder to answer are questions about God's motives. For example, why did God make certain creatures, especially creatures that can hurt us, like bees and snakes? Again, reputable sources (print or online) can teach us something about the values of such creatures. On the other hand, why God wanted the great varieties of flowers, trees, animals, and people is not something that we can answer by means of a search engine! All we can say is that God wanted them all to exist. God seems to like variety! In addition, exactly how all these wonderful creatures came into existence is something that we can't answer, but we can use our imaginations to think of possible ways this might have happened. Encouraging children's imagination will teach them—and us—something about human ideas about God's creativity. This is especially true when a child asks a question (e.g., what cats think about) for which there is no certain answer.

Particularly important is the acknowledgment that God might be continuing to bring new creatures into existence. After all, Scripture says, "See, I am doing something new. Now it springs forth, do you not perceive it?" (Isaiah 43:19). Children are usually quite excited by the idea that God continues to create, even to this day. We should be the same.

The Purposes of Various Creatures

Why did you make bees, ants, plants, sharks, snakes, etc.? (5–8)
Why must there be natural disasters? (11 G)
Why did you make germs? (11 G)
Why did you make the COVID virus that kills people? (14 B)
Why did you make animals that hurt people? (13 B)

Although they are still asking questions to which a concrete answer can be given, older children are much more concerned about God's motives at this age. Questions like those listed above reflect a growing maturity in children's assessment of the world in which they live, a world that is not always safe to inhabit.

Why are there natural disasters? Some people would say that God seems to permit the natural world to just "be," even though that might mean that sometimes bad things happen. In other words, natural disasters occur because creation has a certain freedom, just as human beings do. Certainly, God does not make the natural world bad, just as God does not make bad people. People do bad things because of their misuse of the freedom that God has given them. That is a risk when we give someone freedom to make a choice; they might not choose the best option, and older children and teens understand this because it has undoubtedly happened in their own lives. For example, if a child chooses to stay up late, he will be tired the next day and might not do well on his science test. Children and teens can come up with many other examples. Although the earth doesn't make choices as human beings do, the earth's "freedom" means that it continues to develop. Although human beings might (understandably) see that development as bad (e.g., a volcano eruption or an earthquake), it might not be bad for the earth itself in the long run. More troubling is when people see natural phenomenon, such as earthquakes, tsunamis, and hurricanes, as punishment aimed at certain persons or groups. God doesn't punish people with nature; more likely, it is our own misuse of nature that comes back to haunt us.

Why are there germs? Many germs help us, and our bodies actually have more germs in our bodies than they have cells! Yet, it cannot be denied that some germs inconvenience us, and others make us very sick. In an era of pandemics, this question is very common. Did God create such germs, or did they mutate or change over time to be more virulent? We don't know. What do the children think?

Human Status in All Creation

Are we all alone in the universe? (11 B)
Are we alone? (13–17 B)

Are we alone in the universe? Young people wonder about this because of all the talk of aliens from other planets, with some adults even claiming to see UFOs. So far, no planet that our space program has explored has shown signs of intelligent life, but that doesn't rule out intelligent life beyond our own solar system. God can keep track of living creatures no matter where they are found.

The End of the World

How long will animals live? How long will the earth exist? (6–8)
Will the earth and sun ever collide? (8 B)
Will humans ever become extinct? (11 G)
Are you going to destroy the earth one day? (11 G)
How did the world start and how will it end? (11G)
Will the earth ever explode? (12 G)
How will you end the world? (13 B)

Young people's interest in how the world will end is obvious in this age group. They have the (unrealistic) fear that they will be around when the sun is extinguished or collides with the earth, or when the earth explodes. Reassurance is in order; these events do not seem to be imminent.

God's Imagination vis-à-vis Nature

How did you think up rainbows? (9 G)
How did you design the circulatory system? (11 G)

On the more upbeat side, children's delight in asking how God thought up certain created things (e.g., rainbows, circulatory system) reveal not so much fear of something that will hurt them but awe of God's creativity. These types of questions might be answered with a prayer of praise (or perhaps a psalm, such as Psalm 24, verses 1–2) and encouraging the young person to take a walk in nature, drawing or taking pictures of all the awesome things he or she sees.

SAMPLE CONVERSATIONS

In the following examples, the goal is to permit the child to give voice to his or concerns and questions about nature. Obviously, responses must be matched to a child's age, temperament, and level of cognitive development. In some cases, reassurance is all that is needed; in other cases, a discussion is in order. Each hypothetical conversation is followed by the important points that it is meant to demonstrate.

Five to Eight Years Old

Child: What do animals think about?

Adult: That's a good question. What do you think they think about?

Child: Eating, maybe being petted. Maybe they think about God!

Adult: You might be right! After all, they are God's creatures, too.

In this conversation, a young child's question about animals can be met simply by engaging in the whimsy of the moment.

* * *

Child: Why did God make things that can hurt us?

Adult: Like what?

Child: Bees. Snakes.

Adult: Well, bees and snakes have a role in nature, and God knows that we need them in some way.

Child: But they could hurt us!

Adult: That's true, but they usually don't hurt us if we don't bother them. God doesn't want them to bother us, and God doesn't want us to bother them.

Child: I still don't like them. Do you think that God is still making new things?

Adult: Yes, I do. In the Bible, God even says, "I am doing something new . . . do you see it?"

Child: Wonder what God could be making?

Adult: Maybe a new type of flower. Let's both of us think about it and see if we can come up with some other things God could be making. [Discussion continues]

Young children are often afraid of creatures that could hurt them. In this conversation, a child questions why God would make such creatures, and the adult wisely answers that they probably play some role in nature, a role of which we may be unaware. Obviously, the role of such creatures could be researched, but the point of this example is that we are always discovering something new from the hands (and mind) of God. The adult uses this to further the conversation.

* * *

Child: Do you think there are animals in heaven?

Adult: Why do you ask?

Child: I love my new puppy and I want him to be with me always . . . even when I'm in heaven!

Adult: What kinds of things would you do in heaven with the puppy?

Again, this is a young child thinking imaginatively and the adult joining him in this venture. The child loves his new puppy and wants to be with the puppy forever, and the adult engages the child in that love. Don't make the conversation complicated.

Nine to Twelve Years Old

Child: When do you think the earth will end?

Adult: Why do you ask?

Child: I heard someone say that the sun and the earth would collide and then the earth would explode! All the people and animals would die. The plants, too.

Adult: That's a scary thought, but I don't think that would happen soon. Scientists would tell us if the earth and sun were getting closer together. And they're not. As for when the earth will end, only God knows that.

Child: Well, maybe if there are other creatures on other planets, we could go and stay with them so that we wouldn't die. Do you think that there is life on other planets?

Adult: Maybe, but I don't know. What do you think?

Child: I don't know either, but I hope there's nobody else.

Adult: How come?

Child: Well, if there are too many creatures, God might not be able to know where they all are.

Adult: I don't think so. No matter how many creatures there are, God loves them all.

Child: I sure hope so!

Elementary school–age children are learning a lot about science in school. Questions about when the world will end are common, and reassurance is usually all that is needed. However, this child takes it one step further by thinking of escaping to another planet, where he hopes that there are no other creatures! Obviously, this is not logical, because if there were no other creatures, would the other planets be inhabitable?

Instead of getting into a science lesson, the adult reassures the child that God loves all God's creatures, wherever they may be.

* * *

Child: I'm really bummed out.

Adult: How come?

Child: I heard about an earthquake in Japan, and a lot of people got killed. Why would God allow an earthquake that would hurt so many people?

Adult: I don't know. I do know that sometimes, the earth shifts its position and that causes an earthquake.

Child: Why doesn't God stop the shifting?

Adult: I don't know. What do you think?

Child: I think that God was mad at the people and wanted them to die.

Adult: No, I don't think that's why there was an earthquake. Sometimes, there are earthquakes in places where there are no people. Who was God punishing then?

Child: Hmmm . . . I have to think about that.

The question of why nature can hurt us is a major one for this age group. In this conversation, an elementary school-age child wonders why God let the earthquake (that killed many people) happen. The child concludes that God must have been angry at the people, which the adult identifies as wrong and wisely counters by noting that there have been earthquakes in unpopulated areas. This evokes the child's need to think about his ideas, which is very useful at this age in terms of maturation of thought.

* * *

Child: I heard that a shark bit a lady at the beach.

Adult: That's really sad, isn't it?

Child: Yeah, I bet she was just trying to go for a swim, and the stupid shark bit her.

Adult: Unfortunately, sharks bite.

Child: Why did God make fish that attack even when we're not bothering them?

Adult: What do you think?

Child: Maybe God doesn't want us to have a good time at the beach?

Adult: I don't think that's it at all. I think sharks must be important in nature; that's why they're around.

Child: But they don't have to be so mean.

Adult: Yeah, I wish it didn't have to be that way, too.

Like the earlier example of a young child asking about creatures that can hurt us, this conversation focuses on why a swimmer who was not bothering a shark would get bitten by it. The child wonders if the woman is being punished for having a good time at the beach, something the child may enjoy himself. The adult has pointed out that sharks may have value in nature, but the child still doesn't understand the *why* of an unprovoked attack. All the adult needs to do here is to commiserate with the child and offer reassurance.

Adolescents

Adolescent: I don't understand why God doesn't stop us from ruining the planet.

Adult: What's God supposed to do?

Adolescent: I don't know. Maybe he could punish us somehow.

Adult: I don't think that God works that way. Anyway, God gave us free will.

Adolescent: Yeah, but it shouldn't be used to do bad things.

Adult: I agree, but that's the problem with free will . . . it might be used for the wrong purposes, and, unfortunately, lots of people do that.

Adolescent: If I were God, I would stop people from hurting the earth.

Adult: I'm sure God doesn't like the way that we treat the earth and its creatures. Do you think that there is anything that we can do here at home to protect the earth, to show God that we appreciate what he has given us?

Adolescent: I guess that we could recycle, but how is one family recycling going to save the earth?

Adult: The earth benefits when everyone does his or her part. We can't all do big things, but we can all do the things that are in our power to do.

Ah, free will raises its head again! A teen wants to know why God doesn't stop people from hurting the planet. While the adult offers an explanation of how free will works (noting God's permission for it to do so), the adult furthers the conversation by noting that everyone must do his or her part, which helps the teen to do more than merely bemoan the current situation.

* * *

Adolescent: I saw a crazy story online that a lady came back from being dead. Do you think that's true?

Adult: Well, sometimes, peoples' hearts stop, and they have to be resuscitated. Is that what you mean?

Adolescent: No, the lady said she was dead and saw heaven and all her dead relatives. Can that happen? Can dead people come back after they're really dead?

Adult: If you're really dead for a while, I don't think you can come back.

Adolescent: Why can't we come back? It would be really cool if we could and could tell everyone what really goes on after life here.

Adult: I agree that it would be cool. What do you think goes on after we die? [Discussion ensues.]

As we all know, there are lots of unusual stories on the internet. This teen has seen a "crazy" story about a dead person coming back to life, but while she was gone, she saw heaven. He wants to know if it could be true. The adult gives a rational opinion/explanation, and then furthers the conversation with the teen about what happens after we die. This permits the two to bond and offer some insight into how the teen thinks (and—for the teen—how the adult thinks).

Chapter 8

Children's Questions
about Heaven

Five to Eight Years Old

What's it like in heaven? (5–8)
Where is heaven? (7 G)
Will mean people go to heaven? (7 G)
Will I go to heaven? (7 B)
Will my family be in heaven? Will I get to see them? (8 G)
Can you see people in heaven? (8 G)
How old is heaven? (8 G)

Nine to Twelve Years Old

Is there a heaven? (9–12)
How many people are in heaven? (9–12)
Why is heaven called heaven? (9 G)
Do animals get to heaven? (11 B)
Do people have cancer in heaven? (10 G)
Is anyone turned down for heaven? (11 G)
What kind of life is there in heaven? (12 B)
How long does heaven last? (12 B)

Thirteen Years and Older

Does heaven end? (13 G)

How old are people in heaven? (13 G)
Is the journey to heaven long or instant? (15 G)
Does everyone get to heaven in the end? (16 G)
Is heaven white and cloudy? (17 G)

INTRODUCTION

Christians speak a great deal about heaven, and young people pick up on their words at church services and when someone has died (e.g., "He's in heaven now"). Everyone knows that God is in heaven. But what is heaven, where is it, and who else is in it? Although our faith tradition speaks about "heaven," no one (alive) has seen it. That means we must rely on Scripture to give us an idea of what it's like.

Although Christian theologians think about heaven more as a state of being with God rather than a place, old beliefs, such as heaven is in the sky, die hard. Most adults hope that they will see their loved ones "in heaven" one day, but what does that really mean? Furthermore, there may be some people that we hope we will NOT see in heaven! But where will they be?

Children and teens have the same questions about heaven that many adults do, but their questions are much more concrete. Is a pet in heaven? Is a mean person in heaven? How many people can heaven hold? Does everyone get to go to heaven? Where is it?

With regard to questions about heaven, it is always appropriate to answer questions by saying that no one knows for sure. No one has been to heaven and come back to talk about it. Heaven, however, is a great topic for adults to learn from children and teens what they hope heaven will be. It is a positive topic that is usually full of joy—no suffering or illness; no mean people; seeing loved ones again; perfect happiness.

WHAT THE SURVEYS REVEAL

Children of all ages are interested in the details about heaven—where it is; what it looks like; who is there; whether they will see loved ones there, and so on. As with all questions, the complexity of the answer varies with the age of the child.

Note that no child younger than eight years asked if there was a heaven; young children simply believe it is real. For older children who do question the reality of heaven, we can reassure them that Scripture tells us that there is a heaven, and it is a place of joy and peace because we will be with God who is the Source of joy, peace, and love. People there will not be sad, ill, or have physical deformities. In the Christian faith tradition, heaven is the same as eternal life, but we don't know what that life will be like. Will all of us be adults, or will we be children? We don't know. Will we be the age we were when we died, or will we be the age when we were the happiest? We don't know. What exactly will we do for eternity? Again, we simply do not know. Asking children what they think are answers to such questions is usually enlightening, as we find out what they believe.

Traditionally, although we speak of heaven in the sky (we even call the skies "the heavens") or "up there," we don't know where it is exactly. This answer is necessary for elementary school–age children and teens who know that modern space programs' satellites, space stations, and rockets have gone far into the sky and have not found a "place."

Our faith tradition teaches us that good people go to heaven. That is not a hard concept for children and teens. Yet, some children might wonder if mean or bad people get to heaven, and some teens might wonder if everyone gets to heaven eventually. Obviously, only God knows that answer. Although God is just, God is also merciful. Even though *we* might not permit certain people to enter heaven, God's ways are not ours. Hence, we can't say for certain exactly who is in heaven or how many people are there. Nor can we say anything definite about pets in heaven. Although it might not seem that a faith tradition supports animals in heaven, what God will do for those who love Him surpasses anything that we can imagine.

It is wise to reassure children and teens about loved ones who have died who did not live such good lives. Although we might not think that they could be rewarded for the lives they lived, we do not know how God was working with them in their final moments. Did they repent, like the good thief who was crucified with Christ? Even if the loved ones were unconscious, God could be working with them in the deepest part of their being. We can certainly encourage children and teens to pray for their loved ones who died. And we can also reassure them that, in the next life, they probably will be able to "see" them again, although not with their physical eyes.

Is the journey from death to heaven long or instantaneous? Who can say? Some people who have had near-death experiences have experienced moving along a long tunnel toward a bright light. Although that seems to be instantaneous, we must remember that such individuals did not experience the finality of true death at the time they had the experience. Older children and teens are usually interested in these accounts of near-death experiences, and, occasionally, they have their own accounts to offer.

SAMPLE CONVERSATIONS

In the following examples, the goal is to permit the child to give voice to his or concerns and questions about heaven. Obviously, responses must be matched to a child's age, temperament, and level of cognitive development. In some cases, reassurance is all that is needed; in other cases, a discussion is in order. Each hypothetical conversation is followed by the important points that it is meant to demonstrate.

Five to Eight Years Old

Child: Where is heaven? Who is there?

Adult: Heaven is real, but it's not a place that we can find on a map. Heaven is where God is, and so there has always been a heaven because God has always existed. Heaven is where good people are after they die. They are able to be with God forever.

Child: Someone told me that heaven is in the clouds. But I don't think that's right. Because when the clouds go away, it's just sky. And when astronauts have been in space, they haven't seen God or heaven.

Adult: For a long time, people have talked about heaven being "up" or in the sky. We even call the sky full of stars on a clear night, the heavens. But, you're right. If heaven had been a place that was close to earth, the astronauts would have seen it. Maybe heaven is even farther away. Or maybe heaven is just being with God, like being with your best friend all the time. What do you think of that? [Discussion ensues.]

The young child is so concrete that "heaven" is literally the sky itself, which is why she talks about the clouds and astronauts. The adult gives a simple explanation and furthers the conversation by offering a new, more personal view of heaven, and asks for the child's thoughts about it, giving the adult a window into the child's thinking.

* * *

Child: What do people do in heaven?

Adult: Why do you ask?

Child: I heard we're all going sing and play harps. I don't like harps. I want to play drums.

Adult: Well, I don't know if we're all going to sing and play music, but if we do, I bet you can ask God to let you play the drums.

Child: That would be neat.

The old image of heaven as everyone playing harps doesn't hold much appeal! In this conversation, the young child is not so much interested in what we do in heaven as he is in not playing a harp. The adult permits him to think about playing drums in heaven, an image with which the child resonates. It's a simple conversation that does not need to be complicated.

Nine to Twelve Years Old

Child: Do you think that anyone gets turned down for heaven? Like some bad people?

Adult: It's hard to say who is in heaven and who is not. But someone might not be in heaven if he or she didn't want to be with God forever.

Child: Who wouldn't want to be with God? That would be dumb!

Adult: I think so, too. But because human beings have free will, if they decide that they don't want to be with God, God will honor their decision. I'm sure that doesn't give God any pleasure . . . to know that one of his children don't want to be with him.

Child: Why would God let a bad person into heaven?

Adult: Well, maybe the person was really sorry for what he had done as he was dying, and God forgave him. We don't really know. I hope that every person would want to be with God forever.

Child: Me, too.

Does everyone go to heaven? As elementary school–age children learn history, they learn about atrocities and those who perpetrated them. Will those people get to heaven? The adult in this conversation offers the child an alternate way of thinking—that a person who did wrong in the world was truly sorry before he died. This gives the child something to think more deeply about.

* * *

Child: Will I get bored in heaven?

Adult: I don't think so, but why do you ask?

Child: Our teacher said we would be praising God day and night forever . . . and God might get tired of hearing the same thing over and over. That might get boring. When would we sleep?

Adult: There probably won't be day and night in heaven, so you won't be sleeping. As for what we will do when we're there, I don't know because I've never been to heaven, but I'm pretty sure everyone will be happy and no one will be bored. And I'm sure that God will love hearing us praise and honor him.

Child: I don't want to go to hell, so I want to go to heaven, but I just hope there will be books to read or games to play.

Adult: What else might you like to do in heaven? [Discussion ensues.]

In this conversation, a child (who obviously doesn't like to be bored on earth!) is concerned that heaven might be a boring place; in his child-like imagination, he hopes there will be books to read or games to play. The adult reassures him that heaven will not be boring, God won't get tired of being praised, he won't need to sleep, and everyone will be happy. But, the adult takes the discussion further by asking the child what things he might like to do in heaven, giving the child an opportunity to let his imagination take over.

Adolescents

Adolescent: Do you think that everyone gets to heaven in the end?

Adult: I'm not sure. I know that God is merciful and loving. I know that God wants us all to be with him forever. But I also know that God doesn't force us to be with him if we don't want to. Maybe there have been some people who decided that they didn't want to be with God forever.

Adolescent: We were reading about Hitler in our history class. He killed a lot of people, right?

Adult: Yes.

Adolescent: He could never be in heaven, right?

Adult: From the earliest times of Christianity, people debated about whether everyone would eventually get to heaven, so your question is a good one. Lots of people feel like those who have lived really bad lives should not be rewarded. But that's up to God, right?

Adolescent: Yeah, I guess it's up to God. But I still feel that people who live bad lives shouldn't end up in heaven. I mean, why would God be so unfair to reward a bad person?

Adult: Because God loves all people—both the people who do good things and the people who do bad things. He doesn't like what they do, of course. He is very offended by some human actions. But our faith tradition teaches us that God loves all people because he created them.

Adolescent: That sounds good in theory, but I don't know if I want to be in heaven next to Hitler!

Adult: Who would you like to be next to in heaven? [Discussion ensues.]

One of the earliest heresies in the Christian church is whether bad people could ever get to heaven. Shouldn't God's justice win out over God's mercy? Because of a class lesson, the adolescent in this conversation rails against the idea of a Hitler in heaven. Even the idea of a loving God doesn't quite convince her. While the adult has made her point, she then engages the teen in thinking about who she would like to spend eternity with.

* * *

Adolescent: What age will I be in heaven?

Adult: Come again?

Adolescent: Will I be my age, will I be younger, or will I be older?

Adult: I don't think anyone knows the answer to that question. I don't know that we have a choice or that it matters. But . . . what age would you like to be?

Adolescent: What I am now or a little older.

Adult: Why?

Adolescent: I like the way I am now. What age would you like to be?

Adult: A little younger than I am now.

Adolescent: Why?

Adult: Because that is an age I always liked best.

Adolescent: But will we recognize each other if we're not the age that we remember each other being when we were alive?

Adult: I think we will recognize each other just fine. Remember, we have special knowledge in heaven.

Adolescent: But wouldn't it be weird if a teenager wanted to be an adult, but her father wanted to be a little boy again? How would that work out?

Adult: We won't have ages per se, but it's sure going to be interesting!

We humans imagine ourselves at certain ages; we can't do otherwise because we are wedded to time. In this conversation, the teen asks a sophisticated question about what age we will be in heaven, even offering the example of a teen who might be an adult in heaven while their father is a child! Very imaginative! The fact is that no one knows exactly what happens when we die, so it is all speculation. The adult's comment "It will be interesting" tells the teen that it won't be scary.

Conclusion

In the introduction, I mentioned that the suffering of children and teens prompted me to abandon my faith; I simply could not make sense of it all, given an all-powerful, all-loving God. That lasted ten long years. It was only after children started posing "God questions" to me on medical rounds that I began to think about my faith more maturely than when I left ten years earlier. In a way, children's questions brought me back to my faith.

In hearing their questions, it gave me permission to hear my own. In knowing that I did not have all the answers (nor did I need to), it gave me freedom from the need to be certain at all times. In listening to their questions and struggling to answer them, it reminded me of my younger self but also of my current self—still wondering, still searching, still waiting.

Their questions eventually led me to respect questions more than answers. After all, answers can be scripted; questions are usually more natural. Their questions led me to ponder what I believed and why. For example, why did I believe this but not that?

Surveying thousands of children, I learned the wisdom of several Scripture passages. Isaiah 11:6 says, "A child shall lead them." Such profound questions the surveyed children and teens often posed! Questions without easy answers. Questions for which book learning and higher education provides few answers.

I also learned the wisdom of Jesus's words addressed to his Father: "You have hidden these things from the wise and intelligent and revealed them to little children" (Matthew 11:25). Surveyed children and teens could see beyond the platitudes and niceties and weren't fooled by them. Instead, they drilled deep and encouraged me to do the same.

Once upon a time, it was thought that posing questions was disrespectful to God. After all, who are we to ask God questions? Yet, as I read Scripture more carefully, I found that the most celebrated persons in the Bible often inundated God with questions. From the patriarchs like Abraham and Moses to prophets like Isaiah and Jeremiah to Jesus's disciples and even his mother Mary at the Annunciation, questions are how these figures drew closer to God as they learned more about God.

And why not? Questions are the way humans get to know other humans. "What's your name? Where do you live? What do you do for a living?" It's also the way we learn—both the mundane and the advanced, both in childhood and in adulthood. The children's questions exemplify this. They want to know God; they want to learn more about this God and the world in which they live.

If we can relax with children's questions and not feel as if our credibility is on the line if we can't answer the questions posed, we too can learn more about God and the world. We can learn what's important to children and to us as well. We can draw closer to them and closer to our truest selves.

Although I learned to appreciate and embrace the questions, I began to ask children and teens what they thought an answer might be to the questions they asked before I gave them my opinion. That was *very* helpful, as I learned to really see things from their perspective. I encourage all who work with children and teens to get into the habit of soliciting their opinions before rendering their own.

In fact, there was a question on the original survey that asked, "What do children know about God that grown-ups have forgotten?" It didn't say we never had the information, just that we had forgotten it. The children's answers to this question reveal so much about what they hold dear.

Regardless of age, gender, and Christian denomination, what are the five most common responses?

1. God loves us . . . always.
2. God loves everyone.
3. God is always with us.
4. God always forgives.

5. God made everything.

We'd be wise to permit a bit of "childlike" faith back into our adult ways of seeing things. We'd be wise to renew our understanding of God and God's ways based on the words of young people. What a better world this would be if we could embrace these five responses.

Appendix

Naturally, in a survey of thousands of children, not every question can be included in a book of this length. The following questions, listed by specific question and by age and gender, were the most common ones posed by the children in the survey (marked with asterisks). The age means that numerous children and teens in a particular age bracket posed that question, while the designation "B" (boy) or "G" (girl) indicates which gender was more likely to pose that question. It should be noted that even when a question is listed "6 B" (for example), that does not mean that six-year-old girls did not also pose the question, just that boys were more likely to do so.

These are the types of questions that adults who live with or work with children can expect to hear. They also make good conversation starters when talking with children (individually or in groups), such as "Many children (teens) wonder if God is real; what do you think?"

Very common questions are listed first for each age, followed by other questions that were posed often but less frequently than the preceding questions. Questions are worded exactly as the children and teens worded them; the spelling is faithful to what they wrote as well. After every set of questions, some overall conclusions will be offered. But—be aware—that any given child is unique at every age and might phrase a question in a more (or less) sophisticated manner than children of the same age.

QUESTIONS ABOUT GOD

Five to Eight Years Old

Are you real? (5–8)*
How old are you? (5–8)*
Are you happy [huge]? (5–6)*
What do you do all day? Do you work hard? (5–7) *
Who is your mother and father? (8 G) *
Do you have brothers and sisters? (8 G)*
How do you see us? (5 G)
Are there other gods? (5 G)
How do you disappear? (5 B)
Will you play with me? (6 B)
How many angels do you have? (6 B)
How many names do you have? (6 B)
How are you? (7 B)
Who's your best friend? (7 G)
Are you in our hearts? (7 B)
Why is your name God? (7 G)
Are you coming back? When? (7 B)
What do you look like? (7 B)
How strong are you? (7 B)
How did you think of day and night? (7 G)
Are you friends with everyone? (7 G)
Where do you live? (8 B)
What's your middle name? (8 B)
Do you like to play? (8 B)
Are you always watching over us? (8 B)
What do you do all day? (8 G)
Do you ever get mad? At who? (8 B)
Are you in charge of heaven? (8 G)
How did you pick the 10 commandments? (8 G)
How many people have you healed? (8 B)

Nine to Twelve Years Old

Are you real? (9–12)*
Who is your mother? (10 G)*

Will we ever see you in person? [If you're with us, why can't we see you?] (11 G)*

Are you a man or a woman? (12)*

Can I be God? (9 B)

Who are your parents? (9 G)

Have you been in heaven all your life? (9 B)

What's it like to live in the sky? (9 B)

What do you see when you look at the earth? (9 B)

Why can't we see you? (9 B)

What do you look like? (9 B)

When will you come back? (9 B)

If you came back, what would you do? (9 G)

Do you know the future? (9 B)

Do you hear a lot of prayers? (9 B)

Who inspired you to be holy? (10 G)

In what year were you born? (10 B)

How many good things have you done? (10 B)

What comes after human beings? (10 B)

Where do you really live? (10 B)

How tall are you? (10 B)

Do you still play games? (10 G)

What's your favorite song? (10 G)

What do you really look like? (10 B)

What's your favorite chocolate? (10 G)

Were you born? (11 G)

Who are your parents? (11 B)

What do you look like? (11 G)

How do you make a decision? (11 G)

Do you control weather? (11 B)

Do you always forgive? (11 B)

Is it real, all of it? (12 G)

Can you read minds? (12 B)

Do you like me? (12 B)

If you forgive, why do people go to hell? (12 G)

Will you never leave us? (12 G)

Exactly how old are you? (12 B)

Thirteen Years and Older

Are you real? (13–15)*
Why not appear to shut up non-believers once and for all? (13–17)*
Are you strong? (13 B)
How were you formed? (14 B)
Did you have fun then, now? (14 B)
Do you love everyone? (13 B)
Can anyone be like you? (13 B)
Why can't I hear your voice like some people do? (15 G)

Comment

The questions from younger children are often whimsical, and this does not vary by gender. As young children become older children and teens, the questions become (overall) more probing. As a rule, both girls and boys are interested in God's relationships with other creatures, while boys are more interested in God's powers as they move into adolescence.

QUESTIONS ABOUT THEMSELVES

Five to Eight Years Old

Why are people so mean [nasty, bad] to me [ignore me]? Why can't people be nice to me? (5–8)*
Why do I have to go to school? (6 B)
Why do people ignore me? (6 G)
Is there someone who looks like me? (6 B)
How can I be like you? (7 G)
Why do I have the name I have? (7 B)
Why doesn't friendship last forever? (8 G)
Can you read my mind? (8 G)
Do I have a twin someplace? (8 G)
How can I get a girl to like me? (8 B)
How many pieces of hurt are on my heart? (8 B)

Nine to Twelve Years Old

Am I [have I been] bad? Was I good today? (9–12)*
Will you help me? (9–12)*
Why don't you answer prayers from me? (9–12)*
Why must life be hard [unfair]? (9–11)*
Will you keep me safe [always help me]? (11)*
Can I fly? (9 B)
Why do people pick on me? (9 G)
Do you think I'm stupid? (9 G)
Can you clean my soul? (9 G)
Can I do more to help others? What? (9 G)
What do you want me to do today? (9 B)
Are you always with me? (9 B)
How perfect do I need to be to get to heaven? (9 G)
Can I come back as a kid when I die? (9 G)
Do you always forgive me? (9 B)
Could I change into an animal? (9 B)
Will you do my homework? (9 B)
Can I live to be 399? (9 G)
Am I adopted? (10 G)
Is [NAME] my real friend? (10 B)
What do you like most about me? (10 B)
What do you think of when you think of me? (10 G)
Are you always watching me? (10 B)
Would you send me your picture? (10 G)
Can I perform a miracle? (10 G)
Why do pets die so soon? (10 G)
How do I stop worrying? (10 G)
Was I here before? (10 G)
Am I going up or down? (10 B)
If you say who lives and dies, do you punish the person who kills another? (10 B)
Can I make peace in the world? (10 G)
When will I die so I have time to say goodbye? (11 G)
What is dead like? (11 B)
Will you give me a sign that you're real? (11 B)
Do I pray enough? (11 G)
How long will I be in purgatory? (11 B)

How many sins have I done? (11 G)
Will I go to heaven? (11 B)
Am I good enough? (11 G)
Can I grow up faster? (11 B)
Why can't I go to another school where people will like me? (11 B)
Why did you make me, me? (11 B)
How am I special? (11 B)
Will you help me with my problems? (11 B)
Why has my heart been touched by love but then broken into shards of glass? (11 B)
Will I forget my parents when I die? (12 G)
Will I be remembered when I die? (12 G)
Who are my true friends? (12 B)
Will you help me to succeed? (12 G)
Is my faith too weak? (12 G)
Will you give me telecanesis [telekinesis]? (12 B)
Can I stay alive forever and be young? (12 G)
Why did you pick me to be born when there are millions waiting to be born? (12 G)
Will I have a family when I grow up? (12 B)
Can I be God for a week? (12 B)
Can I have some of your power? (12 B)
Why is my hair oily? (12 G)
Will my secret sins keep me out of heaven? (12 B)
Am I close enough to get into heaven now? (12 G)
Will I be reincarnated? (12 B)

Thirteen Years and Older

What sin have I done the most? (13 B)
What happens to me if I break one of your laws? (13 B)
Why? (13 B)
How can I improve? (13 G)
Is there a plan for me or do things just happen? (16 G)
Is there a pre-destined life partner for me? (17 G)

Comment

Next to the questions about God, the children's and teens' questions about themselves are the next most numerous and very often profound. Relationships with friends are often the subject of questions, as are children's concerns about their future, whether they are being good (enough) to please God, their unanswered prayers, and the difficulties of life. One can almost hear the angst in the child or teen who poses some of these questions.

QUESTIONS ABOUT LOVED ONES

Five to Eight Years Old

Can I talk to Daddy in heaven? (5 B)
Can I go to heaven with mommy? (6 G)
Why can't [NAME] come back to life? (6 G)
Why must my dad work late? (8 G)

Nine to Twelve Years Old

Why does my dad drink so much? (10 G)*
Why do people in my family have babies when they're young? (11 G)
Will my dad lose his job? (11 G)
Why can't I live with my dad? (11 B)
Why can't my dad get a job? (11 B)

Thirteen Years and Older

Why can't my mother forgive and let go of the past? (16 G)

Comment

Both girls and boys have piercing questions about their parents, especially their fathers. Some of these questions may actually be questions about abuse of some kind. Be alert to this.

QUESTIONS ABOUT PEOPLE IN GENERAL

Five to Eight Years Old

How do people grow? (5 G)
Do people come to you for advice? How many? (8 B)

Nine to Twelve Years Old

Do we get two lives? (9 B)
Why can't people fly? (9 B)
How many people believe in you? (10 G)
Are we re-created? (11 B)
Why did you make everyone equal? (11 B)
Are all good people rewarded? (12 G)

Thirteen Years and Older

Why not give people exactly what they want? (14 G)

Comment

Both boys and girls have questions about people in general, with questions about the here-and-now ("Do people come to you for advice?") and the future ("Do we get two lives?").

QUESTIONS ABOUT EVIL AND SUFFERING

Thirteen Years and Older

Why do bad things happen? I want to know from you and not from a textbook. (16 G)
I wouldn't ask a question as I might be scared to know the answer. (16 G)

Comment

Younger children did not explicitly ask about evil, which is a concept that is abstract, especially for younger children, while teens tended to insert themselves into the question.

QUESTIONS ABOUT ILLNESS AND DEATH

Five to Eight Years Old

Why did you invent colds? (7 G)

Nine to Twelve Years Old

Why do you let COVID hang around and keep changing so we can't get rid of it? (9 G)
Do we get a new body in heaven? (10 G)
What do we do during everlasting life? (11 G)
Will everyone get to heaven when they die? (11 B)

Thirteen Years and Older

Why do you take little kids so soon? (13 onward)*

Comment

Older children and teens express more interpersonal concerns, while younger children focus more on the here-and-now of illness.

QUESTIONS ABOUT CREATION

Five to Eight Years Old

What do cats think about? (7 G)
How long did it take to make the solar system? (7 B)
What does the sun look like up close? (7 B)
How long was it before people showed up? (8 G)

Nine to Twelve Years Old

What's at the end of the universe? (9 B)
How did the universe start? (10 G)
How old is the world? (12 B)
Will the ozone layer disappear? (12 B)
Did we evolve from apes? (12 G)
How many fish are there in all the oceans? (12 B)
Do dead things ever live again, come back to life? (12 G)

Thirteen Years and Older

Why do you let us hurt the earth [planet]? (13 G)

Comment

Questions about creation are nearly evenly distributed between girls and boys, with boys' questions more science/fact focused, while girls' questions are more personal.

QUESTIONS ABOUT HEAVEN

Five to Eight Years Old

What's it like in heaven? (5–8)*
Where is heaven? (7 G)
Will mean people go to heaven? (7 G)
Will I go to heaven? (7 B)
Will my family be in heaven? Will I get to see them? (8 G)
Can you see people in heaven? (8 G)
How old is heaven? (8 G)

Nine to Twelve Years Old

Is there a heaven? (9–12)*
How many people are in heaven? (9–12)*
Do animals get to heaven? (11 B)*
Why is heaven called "heaven"? (9 G)

Do people have cancer in heaven? (10 G)
Is anyone turned down for heaven? (11 G)
What kind of life is there in heaven? (12 B)
How long does heaven last? (12 B)

Thirteen Years and Older

Does heaven end? (13 G)
How old are people in heaven? (13 G)
Is the journey to heaven long or instant? (15 G)
Does everyone get to heaven in the end? (16 G)
Is heaven white and cloudy? (17 G)

Comment

As would be expected, younger children's questions about heaven tend to be more personal, while older children's and teens' questions tend to be encompassing. Interestingly, a greater number of girls had questions about heaven (by age and overall) than did boys, perhaps because girls are more invested in relationships and are more attracted to human images of heaven, which often seem more feminine than masculine in nature.

Bibliography

Erikson, Erik. "Eight Stages of Man," in *Childhood and Society*. New York: W. W. Norton, 1985.

Fowler, James, *Stages of Faith: The Psychology of Human Development and the Quest for Meaning*. New York: HarperOne, 1995.

Singer, Dorothy, and Tracey Revenson. *A Piaget Primer: How Children Think*. New York: New American Library, 1996.

About the Author

Dr. Pat Fosarelli, MD, serves on the faculty of the Johns Hopkins School of Medicine in the Department of Pediatrics, and for the last fifteen years she has been chair of the Johns Hopkins Professional Advisory Group, the committee that advises chaplain training at Hopkins. She has also been an associate dean at St. Mary's Ecumenical Institute and is currently director of the St. Mary's MA in Christian Ministries program. At St. Mary's, she teaches in the practical theology and spirituality departments and offers research methodology courses to DMin students. Additionally, she served as a pastoral associate and director of religious education at Corpus Christi Roman Catholic Church (Baltimore) between 2001 and 2008.

In the early 2000s, Dr. Fosarelli regularly contributed as a book reviewer for the *Journal of the American Medical Association* (JAMA). She is the author of twelve books and numerous articles and pamphlets in the medical and theology/ministry fields. Her books include *Paths to Prayer: A Field Guide to Ten Catholic Traditions* (2010); *Celebrating Your Child's First Communion* (2012); *Celebrating Your Child's First Reconciliation* (2012); *Prayers and Rituals at a Time of Illness & Dying: The Practices of Five World Religions* (2008); and others. Dr. Fosarelli currently resides in Baltimore, Maryland.